SPORTING CLAYS

SPORTING CLAYS

An Orvis Guide

◆

Lionel Atwill
with photographs by the author

THE ATLANTIC MONTHLY PRESS
NEW YORK

◆

Published simultaneously in Canada
Printed in the United States of America

Library of Congress Cataloging-in-Publication Data

Atwill, Lionel.
  Sporting clays: an Orvis guide / by Lionel Atwill; with
photographs by the author.
    Includes bibliographical references.
    ISBN 0-87113-390-3
    1. Trapshooting. I. Title.
    GV1181.A89 1990   799.3′13—dc20   90-37054

Design by Laura Hough

The Atlantic Monthly Press
19 Union Square West
New York, NY 10003

FIRST PRINTING

In memory of my godfather, Harry Tietenberg,
who taught me many a lesson in life,
including how to shoot crows from the back of a truck
at thirty miles an hour.

◆

Acknowledgments

◆

My heartfelt thanks to Gary Gras, a double-A shooter and gentleman, who responded to my frequent barrages of questions with humor, grace, and insightful answers; to Bob Philip, whose enthusiasm for this sport knows no bounds and whose backyard course—Bob's Sporting Clays—has no equal; to Rick Rishell, who took the mystery out of gun fit and instinctive shooting for me, as he has for thousands of gunners who've gone through the Orvis Shooting School; to Bill Donohue, who supplied me with all the latest gear; to Tom Rosenbauer and Doug Truax, who came to my aid on numerous occasions; and to all the other good folks at Orvis, always ready with a smile and a helping hand. Also, I'm most grateful to everyone at Sandanona Sporting Clays in Millbrook, N.Y., where I shot many of the photographs for this book. And finally, a wink and a grin to my talented editor, John Barstow, who saw this project through with style and wit.

Without the cumulative help of these folks, this book never would have yelled "Pull!"

Contents

◆

Introduction

◆

Life is far too important a thing
ever to talk seriously about.
—OSCAR WILDE

I shoot birds.

I shoot them passably well—when the gods are with me, which happens occasionally toward the end of the season on my home turf. If I had to be objective about my shooting (and this is as impossible as being objective about one's performance in that most popular indoor sport), I'd say I'm average, although my ego would wage that I might outshoot you (if you're average) while hunting my birds—grouse and woodcock—in my backyard.

I've been shooting birds for thirty years. Quail in Georgia and Texas and Kansas. Pheasant in South Dakota and Utah and, once, in South Korea, where I was the exotic and the birds were the natives. Dove in South Carolina and Texas. A whole pile of woodcock, a smaller pile of grouse, the occasional chukar, one prairie chicken, two sharptail, and never, but never, a partridge in a pear tree.

In an apple tree, once or twice, but they deserved it.

1

I mention this to let you know that I am not a big shooter of pigeons—clay pigeons, that is. At least not the organized kind of clay pigeon shooting most Americans do—trap or skeet.

When I was a kid I learned to shoot a shotgun during my twelfth summer by firing innumerable rounds at clay pigeons tossed by friend and relatives, first from a hand trap and later, as my gunning improved, from a mechanical slinger mounted on a massive platform of two-by-sixes that resided in the field behind our house.

By my thirteenth summer my casual clay pigeon shooting had evolved into a larger ritual. Every Sunday after church, my stepfather and his assorted cronies would gather behind the house to "bust pigeons." This statement indicated a certain degree of optimism, for many a pigeon lived to be flung another day.

Since my enthusiasm for shotguns had spawned this rite, I was invited to participate, with the proviso that after the shoot I would pick up the hulls and gather the surviving birds that littered the mowed field like an invading force of tiny spaceships.

Inspired by the opportunity to best my elders (and to reduce the number of space invaders, the gathering of which took an hour of my afternoon), I became a good shot.

The challenge was, by most standards, quite pedestrian as was our shooting. The gunner stood to the left of the trap. He would fire ten shots, then move to the trap to throw birds for the next man in line. With this setup, all the birds were straight away or mildly quartering—eighthing or sixteenthing would be more accurate terms.

Two summers later, when I was fifteen, I no longer missed these simple shots; unfortunately, neither did the adults. So I changed the rules. I varied the gunner's position. I insisted everyone start with the gun not mounted, but in the ready position, as I had been taught to shoot, in anticipation of a bird's flush. I decreed that the trapper could fling the pigeon whenever he wished once the gunner said he was ready; there would be no cry of "Pull!" I fiddled with the trap's adjustments, installed a hot spring pirated from a piece of farm machinery, and discovered that I could skim a bird low to the ground for one shot and follow with another that soared to the heavens. I got pretty good at throwing those birds and just as good at shooting them, good enough to take some pocket change from the grown-ups, good enough to establish basic wingshooting skills that have served me well over the years.

I shot skeet a couple of times after I reached adulthood, but it never gave me much of a tingle. Nor did trap. That's a comment on me, certainly, not on those games, for they have many avid devotees who find challenge and satisfaction aplenty in both. It is all a matter of taste.

◆

About eight years ago, I shot some clay pigeons for the first time in fifteen years. I had fun doing it, too. The occasion was the thirty-ninth birthday of my friend Geoff. Being a sensible man, Geoff swore that his thirty-ninth would be the last birthday he'd celebrate. Given that edict, his wife, who enjoys putting on a fête whenever she can, came up with a plan for the Thirty-ninth Anniversary Sporting Classic, a three-event extravaganza.

Geoff and a dozen of his friends assembled at dawn in front of Mother Murphy's Donut Shop, where we were issued T-shirts emblazoned with SPORTING CLASSIC, a large coffee, three donuts of our choice, and the rules. We would leave the parking lot in a Le Mans mass start and proceed to the fabled Battenkill River, where we'd fish for exactly one hour. Catch in hand, we'd then return to Geoff's house for a check-in, a measuring of fish, more coffee, and assorted sweet rolls. Next, we'd shoot an archery course I'd laid out in the woods, followed by more coffee and beignets. Finally, full of calories and caffeine, we'd move to a hillside from which we would attempt to kill flushing grouse—actually clay pigeons launched from a trap artfully hidden in the woods. Each event would count for so many points. The competition would be capped with a four-course champagne breakfast.

The unimportant issue is who won. The winner garnered the

coveted Sporting Classic Coffee Cup not by showing prowess with gun and bow but by catching *one* fish—the only fish taken, an emaciated six-inch brook trout.

Such are the wiles of the fabled Battenkill. And such is the fickleness of sporting competitions.

The important thing I remember is the success of the grouse shoot. The food was good, the archery amusing, but the wingshooting was a hoot. First, the targets were new to all the competitors; the knowledgeable, grooved skeet or trap shooters among us had no advantage here. Second, the clays simulated birds, and, to a man, we were bird shooters. And finally, this was the most sociable event.

Had I the sense most pointing dogs are born with, I would have recognized that a wonderful game was hiding within those simulated flushing grouse. I would have seen the beginning of what has grown to be a wave of enthusiasm for the newest shooting sport to sweep this country.

Such is life. These things slip by us. Had I been perceptive I would have realized I was shooting an abridged form of this game almost thirty years ago, when I was fifteen years old.

◆

The game I failed to recognize, of course, is sporting clays. I missed my chance to claim it, but fortunately, a few years later, the Orvis Company saw the appeal of the sport in England, where its roots go deep, and brought it to America.

Now we all have a chance to enjoy sporting clays for the same reasons my friends and I enjoyed our simulated grouse shoot eight years ago (and for the same reasons I so loved shooting clay pigeons as a kid): the game simulates shooting real birds; it shows you targets you've never seen before, making every outing a new challenge; it's relatively simple to set up; it's shootable throughout the year; and it's as sociable as any shooting sport can be, perfect for introducing new shooters of any sex or age to the gun.

Simply put, sporting clays has more fun to it—more *game* in it—than any other shooting sport.

Introduction

Sporting clays for the fun of it is what this book is about. Since I've already told you I missed two obvious opportunities to become the American guru of this game, I doubt I could convince you that I'm among the top sporting clays shooters in the country, if not the world.

But I won't try, because I don't have to. I have co-conspirators here, so my prowess with a gun need not come to the fore. I live next door to the Orvis Company, and I know the people who work there—gunsmiths, instructors at their renowned shooting school, casual clay shooters, serious competitors, the folks who work in the store, the people who market and manage and otherwise run the show. Collectively, they have an impressive body of knowledge about the game: guns, traps, shells, techniques, teaching methods, gun fit, gear. Orvis is America's adoption agency for sporting clays, and it is therefore fitting that they conspired with me to write this book.

This guide is organized in a straightforward manner. You can skip around, if you like, but I'd suggest you read the chapter on wing-shooting before you read those chapters dealing with the guts of the game. I say this because good wingshooting technique is fundamental to doing well at sporting clays; even if you don't plan to compete, you'll want to do well and best your friends.

I've been shooting for a good while and had never recognized how many poor habits I'd developed until I spent some time with a competent instructor at the Orvis Shooting School. I adhere to the techniques they teach, as do the English schools. The majority of the top British shooters, who represent the majority of the best sporting clays gunners in the world, follow their methods, too, with only minor modifications in very special cases.

If you are new to shooting, please find a qualified, even-tempered instructor to teach you gun safety and shooting basics. The careful handling of a gun is not something you can learn from a book. Practice safe gun handling all the time. The maxim "Treat any gun as loaded" may sound trite, but it is critical advice. Failure to heed safe gun-handling practices results in much worse than embarrass-

5

ment. Sporting clays may be compared to the game of golf, but that comparison ends with the subject of safety. There is nothing more serious than a loaded gun.

Trapper ready?

Then turn the page and pull.

1

What Is This Thing Called Sporting Clays?

◆

*The fascination of shooting as a sport
depends almost wholly on whether
you are at the right or wrong end of the gun.*
—P. G. WODEHOUSE

Golf is the analogy of choice used to describe sporting clays. The obvious similarity is that both are played out over courses composed of individual stations that differ substantially from one another; those variations are achieved by integrating the terrain into the design of each station. Both golf and sporting clays are also nearly impossible to master.

The comparison holds on other levels, too, the first being that both games can involve a wide range of activities. As golf can run the gamut from pitch-and-putt to the Masters, so too can sporting clays encompass everything from a one-trap backyard setup to the United States Sporting Clays Association (USSCA) or the National Sporting Clays Association (NSCA) top-of-the-heap championships.

Basically, sporting clays is a shotgun shooting game in which clay pigeons are presented to the gunner in ways that approximate the flight pattern of game birds (and occasionally game rabbits) in their natural habitats. On all but the simplest courses, the shooting grounds are laid out in stations (also called stands or butts, the British term), with each station representing one type of bird or a combination of game (a rabbit and a grouse, for example). At each station, clay pigeons are usually thrown in pairs, five or so pairs to the station. A course consists of several stations, usually five or ten, but fewer or more are permissible. One hundred birds or more may be presented over the course.

Sometimes birds from the same traps may be shot from different positions, so the gunner sees the same targets from entirely different angles, which creates entirely new shooting problems. An area presenting pigeons to several stations from a single trap is called a field.

Given the variations in trap position, trap speed, shooting position, and flight paths of different types of clay pigeons, targets can come through the trees, from under your feet, straight down your throat, over your head, quartering, going away, left to right, right to left, and in any other path a real bird might choose.

Which means any path at all.

They can tower, drop, twist, quiver. They can fly fast or slow, high or low. About the only thing they can't do is accelerate.

The key words here are *unpredictable, variable,* and, as you will learn, bordering on *impossible.*

As in golf, the rules of sporting clays become more specific, and therefore more restrictive, as the level of competition increases. There are a few basic rules, however, that define the sport:

- The gun may not be mounted but must be held off the shoulder with the entire butt visible beneath the arm, and the shooter may not mount his gun until he sees the targets.
- Only two shells may be loaded.
- If doubles are tossed and both are broken with one shot, both are counted as kills.
- A malfunction of the gun is counted as a lost bird under USSCA rules; the NSCA allows two malfunctions per day without penalty.

◆ Chokes or guns may be changed only between fields. A field is
one or more shooting stations serviced from a common trap. The
NSCA permits chokes to be changed between stations.

You'll notice that the natural laws of bird shooting have been
translated, more or less, into the rules of sporting clays.

Several other elements come into play at all but the backyard
level, but these are the fundamental rules. As with the rules of any
good game, they provide a framework with ample room for movement in many directions.

ROOTS

The roots of wingshooting for sport go back to the time of the *Iliad;*
Homer speaks of the grand pastime of shooting a pigeon tethered
by a string to the top of a mast. The weapon of choice was the bow
and arrow; the challenge, obviously, was significant.

Wingshooting with a shotgun had its origins in England in the
mid–eighteenth century, paralleling the refinement of the black
powder shotgun. In the nineteenth century, live pigeon shoots became popular, reaching their peak toward the end of the Victorian
era, when one's ability to handle a gun had definite social implica-
tions.

The popularity and respectability of pigeon shooting waned in
the early part of this century. Fortunately, George Ligowski, an
American, invented a replacement for live birds in 1880. Made of
baked clay and modeled after the clamshells he had seen boys skim
across the water, Ligowski's "clay pigeon" quickly replaced feather-
filled glass balls—the older inanimate alternative to real birds—and
just as quickly replaced the real thing.

The first clay pigeon game, which imitated live pigeon shooting,
was called trap, after the device used to hold and release live birds.

In 1926, a new shooting game evolved in Massachusetts, designed to approximate the fast, close-range shooting found in New England grouse coverts. In a contest sponsored by the game's inventors, the name skeet, from the Scandinavian root word for "shoot," was bestowed on the sport by a Montana lady of Norwegian ancestry. And skeet it has remained.

Meanwhile, back in England, shotgunning continued to be a popular pastime and ability to handle a gun a skill of some significance. The demand to perform at estate shoots on driven game gave rise to a number of shooting schools. These schools, in turn, adapted Ligowski's lowly clay pigeon to use on practice fields of targets that approximated the flight of live quarry, as the English like to call it. Sporting clays was born.

Although the British Open, England's premier sporting clays competition, dates back to 1925, sporting clays has made its greatest gains in popularity in England within the last twenty years. (The sport was not yet well enough established to deserve mention in the 1971 revised edition of Macdonald Hastings' classic English shooting book, *Robert Churchill's Game Shooting.*)

Back in the States, skeet and trap have held their own over the last two decades, but neither sport made significant inroads among mainstream bird shooters—waterfowlers, upland gunners, dove shooters, and the like.

Recognizing this, and sensing a need for an instructional shooting program pitched to the bird shooter rather than the competitive trap or skeet gunner, the Orvis Company started a shooting school in 1973 at the company's headquarters in Manchester, Vermont. Orvis sent several of the better shots on its staff to the top English schools. These soon-to-be instructors returned not only with teaching techniques that would evolve into the modified Churchill Method taught at Orvis today (more on this later), but also with ideas for a shooting-ground layout based on what they had seen in England. What they had seen, of course, was the progenitor of contemporary American sporting clays.

The Orvis Shooting School course began with a duck tower, a wobble trap, several automatic traps that could be used from different shooting positions, and a quail walk, a path lined with hand-cocked traps tripped by a long chain pulled by the instructor. (The quail walk would become the Neanderthal cousin of American sporting clays, very close to the game that ultimately emerged but not quite right and therefore squashed, in the evolutionary sense, by the fickle foot of the shooting public.)

In a few years the Orvis shooting ground was almost—but not quite—a sporting clays course. To use the golf analogy one more time, Orvis had a five-hole course (with no sand traps, no water hazards, and no tees) in what would become a nine-hole game.

In 1983, Orvis asked Bryan Bilinski, the manager of Orvis's Houston retail store, to set up an Orvis shooting school in Texas. Admitting that he knew next to nothing about shooting schools, Bryan wanted to go to England to see what the real thing looked like. And off he went.

He returned to Houston with a vision: instead of building a layout tailored strictly for shooting instruction, Bryan wanted to put in a true sporting clays course, with shooting stations built to simulate the flight of game birds and designed to be shot for fun.

"I stuck my neck out," he recalls. "But I knew the Houston market. Those guys would rather shoot than do anything else. Anything. But a lot of them were soured on trap and skeet. They were hunters, but they felt intimidated shooting those games against experienced trap and skeet shots."

Bryan built the Orvis Houston Shooting School with bark-mulched pathways between stations, with names for each of the six positions, and with many of the features of field shooting, save for real birds.

That fall, Bryan hosted a charity fun shoot for a local Ducks Unlimited chapter. "About seventy-five guys turned up. Some had skeet guns, some had trap guns, but a lot were dragging field guns. These were people who had given up on clay pigeon games. But at the end of the day, I saw a lot of them giggling like school kids, regardless of whether they had hit anything during the shoot. Then I knew we had something."

The following year, 1985, Orvis hosted the first national sporting clays championship at its Houston facilities, for which the company established the Orvis Cup. "Several shooters at that competition paid us the highest compliment," says Bryan (now the publisher of Countrysport Press in Traverse City, Michigan). "They went home and set up sporting clays courses."

Sporting clays had come to America.

◆

Throwing clay pigeons in ways that simulate the flight of game birds is not a novel idea. I was doing it back in the fifties; if you're a bird shooter, you probably did it in one form or another when you were learning to shoot, too. But you and I failed to codify that informal shooting, to set a few rules, to give shape and form to the game. "I made up most of the rules for that first shoot," says Bryan. "My principal guideline was the fact that the game must emulate field shooting. For example, I said that the maximum load that could be used was one ounce of shot. That permitted a guy shooting a twenty-gauge to compete against a guy shooting a twelve without too much of a handicap. I'm sorry to see that competitive sporting clays has gone to a one and one-eighth ounce load maximum. Maybe that will change. [England recently limited shot loads to one ounce.]

"I also set up categories for side-by-sides and for sixteen-, twenty-, and twenty-eight-gauges. I hope the sport comes back to that. I hope it doesn't get too far away from its field shooting heritage."

Codifying the game helped pave the way for sporting clays' grand entrance; to a lesser degree, so did the times. America was ripe for the importation of such a perceptibly English game.

Americans have always been closet Anglophiles. We like the pomp and ceremony, the royalty, the style of the English landed class; in Sporting Clays, we've found a way to simulate that style. All these years we've watched the royals prowling the moors in their heavy tweeds, weathering the foul English weather in their Barbour jackets ("The best British clothing for the worst British weather!"), blasting away at driven bird after driven bird. Well, sporting clays has provided us with a way of doing most of that without having to understand cricket or eat overcooked vegetables or the innards of sheep.

◆

Before leaving this lofty plane of the social and historical significance of shooting a pitch platter with a shotgun, let's dwell for a moment on the very name of the sport.

After Orvis introduced America to the game, there was an awkward year or two as we came to grips with the slightly snobbish name: *sporting* almost begs for an affected, nasal, uppercrust accent.

There is only one -ing word I can think of that trips easily off the American tongue. Gerunds are not our meat. Hunter's clays was tried for a while, but that confused shooters all the more: were there two games here or one with two names? It's unfortunate that someone didn't sponsor another contest to name this newest shooting game. Almost anyone could have come up with something less affected than sporting clays. Nevertheless, the game is now named. Sporting clays it is and sporting clays it shall remain.

WHAT MAKES IT FUN
◆

Wearing wellies and a Barbour waxed jacket may be neat, but that's not what makes sporting clays so appealing. Nor is the fact that targets approximate birds the only plus to the game. Sporting clays scores high on a number of levels.

First, sporting clays is out and out unabashed fun. It lets you have some laughs shooting a round in a very social environment. Because there should never be a perfect score recorded on a decent course, missing doesn't carry the stigma in sporting clays that it does in trap or skeet, so we bird hunters, who are apt to miss at clay targets from time to time, are less intimidated. We relax, we laugh, and, as an added bonus, we often shoot better.

Sporting clays will never replace an armpit sport—football, baseball, basketball, and the like—as a spectator's game of choice, but as shooting games go, it's not bad to watch. A gallery often forms around a group of shooters, following them from one station to the next in a mildly raucous mob. That makes the game all the more sociable.

Second, sporting clays can be a wonderful head game for those who enjoy psychological battles. Normally, a string of three to five gunners will shoot one station at a time. The first shooter is afforded a chance to see the targets before shooting his round. Subsequent shooters get to watch. And watch. And watch. That can be good, to a point. It also can be nerve-wracking. The more you intellectualize a game like this, the more difficult it becomes. There is ample opportunity for a shooter to talk himself out of a decent score before he chambers his first round. This factor may be important to some; it does not, however, need to dictate the game.

Third, and most important, sporting clays offers infinite variety, making it appealing to both the beginner and the experienced shooter. Variety also heightens the competitive side of the game. In trap or skeet shooting, where the top competitors practice a highly grooved style, hundreds of birds may be thrown before the winner is separated from the pack. Not so in sporting clays. Fifty birds will often do it; a hundred always will.

This wonderful variety is the result of a number of factors, the most obvious of which are listed here.

Terrain: A well-designed course takes advantage of gullies, hills, draws, ponds, and other physical features to simulate birds' natural environment. A good course also uses vegetation. A quartering grouse may be relatively easy to hit until a maple tree enters the equation.

Trap Location and Speed: Since sporting clays courses are most often set up with relatively simple and mobile manual traps, the location of the traps can easily be varied. And by tightening a spring, the speed of birds can be changed from day to day.

Target Selection: Currently, five targets are used on most sporting clays courses: standards, 108-mm diameter, run-of-the-mill clay pigeons; midis, 90-mm pigeons; minis, the trolls of the clay pigeon family, only 60 mm in diameter; battues, which look like pancakes and fly about the same; and rabbits, heavyset pigeons designed to withstand the bumps and bruises inherent in bouncing on the ground. But as other targets are invented, they'll make their way into the lineup. Current USSCA rules stipulate that 64 percent of the targets thrown must be standard clay pigeons.

Shooting Position: A gunner may walk up a station (that is, he may be in motion when the birds are released), but on most sporting clays courses the man or woman on the line shoots from a stationary position. Most often this firing position is defined by a cage of some sort, which limits the swing of the gun. This is a safety precaution first and foremost, but it is also a variable, for it forces you to shoot within a limited arc. Not all shots are taken from a standing position, either. There are stations designed to be shot from pit blinds, from bobbing layout boats, from under tree limbs. Shooting position is limited only by the imagination of the course designer.

Background: Contrast between targets and background can vary with changes in the light, changes in the color of the birds, and changes in the season. A bright orange target against a line of leafy trees is easy to see on a clear summer day. But on a cloudy January afternoon, when the leaves have dropped and the sky is hangover gray, that same bird is more difficult to pick out. Change the bird from orange to white and it may disappear. Change the bird back to orange and paint the background with fall leaves, and the picture changes again.

Timed Reloads: On some stations a set length of time is allocated between reloads, which forces the shooter to load quickly and compose himself for the next pair of birds. The additional pressure of reloading is an interesting variable. Most bird hunters are accustomed to reloading rapidly; clay target shooters are not.

Doubles: Herein lies the rub of sporting clays. A good shot could break most of the targets thrown on a sporting clays course if those targets came out one at a time. But that's rarely the case. Pairs of targets are most often thrown, and recovering quickly from the first shot and getting on the second shot is one key to succeeding at sporting clays.

Pairs of targets are presented in one of three manners: simultaneous pairs, in which both birds are thrown at the same time; report pairs, in which the second bird is launched on the sound of the gunner's shot at the first bird; and following pairs, in which the second bird is launched after a brief delay, usually the amount of time needed to recock and reload the trap.

Two different birds may be launched in a pair; a report pair might consist of a standard followed by a midi.

Delayed Launch: On any given station the trapper may elect not to release the birds for up to three seconds after the gunner calls "Pull!" Three seconds is up about the moment you drop your gun, turn to your shooting pals with a quizzical look, and say, "The kid must be asleep at the trap."

Poison Birds: A poison or hen bird, representing a protected sex or species, may be designated. Such a bird will be of a different color than the regular clay birds thrown. A shot at a poison bird, whether the shot hits or not, constitutes a miss. Keeps you honest. Poison birds also placate those who think a pigeon is an endangered species.

Add up all those variables and you'll understand the challenge of sporting clays. The game changes its look more often than Cher. And as shooters improve their skills, so do course designers. Remember, a perfect score—one hundred out of one hundred, even fifty out of fifty—demonstrates a flaw in the course, not excellence behind the gun.

There is much talk about the similarities between game birds and sporting clays but little about the differences. And they do exist. Real birds accelerate in the air; clay pigeons decelerate. The shooter faces a far greater physical challenge in hunting than in shooting targets, and he is rewarded with an experience that has few equals.

Nevertheless, sporting clays comes as close to the shooting experience of hunting as any game ever will. As more courses are built and more hunters enter the ranks, we'll see changes in the game that will skew it all the more toward field shooting, toward the hunter rather than the competitive shot. We'll see more gunners shooting twenty-gauge and even twenty-eight-gauge guns, and that will give way to designated classes for the smaller bores. We'll see more walking stations. I wouldn't be surprised to see a field set up with one station at the bottom of a hill and another at the top and a time limit imposed on moving from one station to the other, building physical challenge into the game.

The options are endless.

As we explore this new game, we all must remember another lesson from the game of golf. This cardinal rule was best stated in a *Golf Magazine* article by Jim Murray, in which he notes, "Golf is the most overtaught and least-learned human endeavor. If they taught sex the way they teach golf, the race would have died out years ago."

Shooting is an intuitive sport. There are fundamental rules that make better shots out of most of us, but there is also a point beyond which all the talk in the world will do no good.

The best way to learn sporting clays is to get out there and do it. Enjoy yourself, have a few laughs, improve your bird shooting. Don't intellectualize the game to death. Don't approach recreation with the intensity of Donald Trump swinging yet another deal.

2

Guns and Shells

◆

This is my rifle and this is my gun,
One is for fighting, the other's for sporting clays.
—JAMES JONES, on first
shooting sporting clays

You don't need a lot of stuff to shoot sporting clays, but you do need a gun, and the best gun to use is the gun you use best. More often than not, that will be the gun you shoot most frequently or the gun that fits you best. (Good fit and frequent use are not synonymous, however. Just because you can hit with the thing doesn't necessarily mean it fits you properly. It may mean you've learned to contort yourself to fit the gun. See chapter 5 for more on fit.)

So start with your favorite hunting gun. If you have several, use the one you most enjoy. If your ego is on the line, pick a twelve-gauge with an open choke. If you have confidence in a smaller gauge and someone else's ego is on the line, try a sixteen-, twenty-, or even a twenty-eight-gauge.

If you own a gun with twenty-eight-inch barrels—a waterfowling gun, rather than a shorter barreled upland gun—all the better. That extra length will smooth out your swing on longer shots. Don't worry about anything else for the moment. You're sufficiently gunned for your initial foray.

After you've popped off a round or two of sporting clays, you'll realize that you miss more than you think you should; the time has come to bear down and get your equipment in order. You may wish to modify the gun you own. The first step is to see that it fits correctly (chapter 5). The second may be to adjust the choke. The third is to play with the weight of the gun (see the section on weight in this chapter). If all that fails, you might want to consider a dedicated sporting clays gun. If all that works, you still might consider a dedicated sporting clays gun. After all, everyone can use at least one more gun.

THE DEDICATED SPORTING CLAYS GUN
◆

Dedicated, in this sense, doesn't mean a gun designed specifically for sporting clays. On the contrary, a good sporting clays gun is a shooter and should serve you pretty well in the field, particularly for game like dove or waterfowl, where passing shots are frequent and the walking distance is measured in feet, not miles (sporting clays guns are a bit heavy for grouse or quail). In fact, there is a good chance a new sporting clays gun will shoot nicer patterns and be more versatile than whatever you're using now, because a good sporting clays gun is, first and foremost, a gun that fits well and can adapt to varying conditions.

A word of warning is in order here: marketing plays a substantial role in the gun trade, and when a new shooting game comes along, manufacturers are quick to jump on the bandwagon with a new gun designed expressly for the new sport—or so they would like you to think. In truth, some of the dedicated sporting clays guns I've seen are clunky, ugly affairs. Don't leap to buy a gun because of the glowing description in the ads. Try it out. Heft it. Shoot it, if you can.

A field gun may be more to your liking than a gun emblazoned with a sporting clays label.

Now let's look at the variables from action through butt.

Action

Single shot and bolt action shotguns are not for shooting things in the air, not if you're over twelve years old.

Pump guns are dependable, inexpensive stalwarts. They probably have accounted for more game in America than any other kind of shotgun. But for sporting clays, they have drawbacks. First, a single-barreled pump doesn't offer a choice of chokes on successive shots, and being able to have an open choke for the first shot and a slightly tighter choke for the second can be important. Second, and more significant, is the need to shuck a pump after the first shot. This tromboning action can disrupt your concentration and interrupt a smooth swing for that important second target, particularly if you haven't run a lot of shells through your pump. There are a bunch of hunters out there who can work a pump's action faster than an automatic without a perceptible hitch in their timing or swing. Some pump aficionados say the delay of working the action keeps them from rushing that second shot. If you like pumps and are comfortable with them, don't discount using one for sporting clays.

The automatic is America's gun, and an automatic works very well for sporting clays. With its single barrel, it's at the same disadvantage as a pump in the choke department, but that small handicap has been overcome a time or two. Of the two reported instances in which a sporting clays gunner shot a perfect one hundred out of one hundred birds, one round was shot with the ubiquitous Remington 1100, the auto for all seasons.

The action of an automatic absorbs some of the perceived recoil of the gun, which can be a distinct advantage over a hundred-bird day. The hunter who pops off a dozen shells in an afternoon, each fired in the flurry of a flush, never feels recoil. But put that same gunner on a sporting clays course and have him fire a hundred shells, a dozen or so of which go off before the gun is well mounted, and he will be painfully aware of recoil. An automatic eases that pain.

The downside of the automatic is its habit of occasionally malfunctioning if not adequately cleaned (or, in the case of some guns, if cleaned too thoroughly). This is a peccadillo that many trap and skeet shooters and bird hunters have overcome. Some shooters of automatics, I believe, take a perverse pride in being able to maintain their guns so that they never malfunction. The threat of a failure is a challenge to them.

Traditionally, the double-barreled shotgun is the gun for sporting clays. Since the game has its roots in the English shooting schools, the side-by-side was, initially, the gun of choice, and the side-by-side is still a good gun. A side-by-side offers two shots with virtually no chance of malfunction short of total mechanical failure. A side-by-side is a quick-pointing, smooth-swinging gun that lends itself well to the instinctive style of shooting demanded of the bird hunter and the sporting clays shooter. A side-by-side sits comfortably in your hands, balances beautifully, and, when well fitted, points where you look as naturally as a jutting index finger. A side-by-side can also offer a different choke for the second shot.

Then why doesn't everyone use one? Cost is one factor. Side-by-sides are more expensive to build than over-and-unders, in part because side-by-sides have never been marketed effectively to Americans; consequently, the demand for them has always been slight. Further, side-by-sides rarely have interchangeable choke tubes, so unless you travel with a gunsmith, the chokes you start with on a round will have to see you through the course. (A truly elegant shooter would overcome this obstacle by carrying a brace, if not a trio, of side-by-sides; at the very least, he'd bear several sets of barrels. Any reasonable course official would award him a dozen dead targets on style alone.)

Having a barrel lying on either side of the sight rib is disconcerting to many shooters who have grown up with single-barreled guns, although those who have shot a side-by-side for any time at all adapt quickly and often come to favor the broad breadth of barrel swinging in front of them.

Finally, a side-by-side usually balances farther back toward the action than an over-and-under. This makes for quick handling in the coverts but a little too quick, many feel, for some of the longer shots encountered in sporting clays.

At the first sporting clays shoot Orvis sponsored in Houston, a separate class was established for side-by-side guns. That classification fell by the boards during the early days of the sport, but as more and more hunters come into the game, I believe we'll see a resurgence of interest in a side-by-side class, just as we'll see classes open up for the smaller gauges. I'd also venture that, with practice, any one of the top sporting clays shooters could shoot as well with a side-by-side as with an over-and-under.

Like pro tennis players, however, the top guns in this game are sponsored. They shoot the shotguns that are given to them, and the ones that are given to them are the guns the manufacturers believe will appeal to consumers. That rules out most side-by-sides, which are either too expensive or too difficult to obtain. If Purdey or Holland and Holland—or any one of the other top-quality side-by-side makers—would like to sponsor a shooter, I'm available. Please send your full line for evaluation. When I'm finished, I'll call you.

As you've guessed by now, the action of choice in this game is the over-and-under. An over-and-under is reliable, easy to load, and offers two quick shots and a choice of two chokes at any one station (plus an infinite variety when fitted with choke tubes). Over-and-unders are more readily available and, by and large, far less expensive than side-by-sides.

An over-and-under balances farther toward the muzzle than a side-by-side and weighs a bit more, qualities that smooth your swing on crossing birds and distant targets. Competitive shooters claim that the recoil of the first barrel of a side-by-side causes the gun to jump laterally a bit. This lateral shift is a distraction to the shooter who must quickly pick up and swing through a second target on doubles. An over-and-under is more immune to this sideways jump, because the barrels are inherently stiffer and are lined up with the stock. Since the lower barrel, which is most closely aligned with the center axis of the stock, is usually the first fired, the recoil of the first shot is directed all the more straight back, in line with the shooter's shoulder. The result is less lateral muzzle jump, which allows the gunner to get on the second target quickly.

Contemporary over-and-unders can usually shoot steel shot, too, so your sporting clays gun can double up in a goose or duck blind. Finally, the heft and look of an over-and-under, with its single sight plane and pistol grip, is more familiar to most American shooters, whose initiation into shooting sports usually occurs with a rifle of similar conformation.

The over-and-under shares an important trait with the side-by-side that I, as a bird hunter, find particularly comforting: a quick glance at the gun tells me when it is absolutely safe—that is, incapable of firing. When I can see a double-barrel bent in the middle, I rest easy. Automatics and pumps, unloaded and with their actions open, don't offer the same clear visual signal.

At a sporting clays event, lots of armed people will be strolling about from station to station. It's reassuring to see their guns broken. An unloaded automatic is no more dangerous, of course, than a broken double, but from forty feet away I don't know if that automatic is unloaded like I do when I see a double broken in half. Further, the person carrying the gun has absolutely no doubt about whether or not there is one more shell in the magazine.

As more neophyte shooters enter the game, gun safety will become increasingly important. A broken double quickly confirms that all is in order.

So much for action. Let's look at the other attributes of shotguns. The variables we'll discuss all apply to over-and-unders, that being the action of choice. Many of these variables apply to other actions,

A broken gun is clear indication of a safe gun. This is a good way to carry a gun from station to station.

too, so don't run off in a huff because the only gun you own and ever plan to own is a fifteen-year-old Remington 1100. Remember that perfect score shot with the venerable automatic. Remember too that all the minor trappings we're about to discuss—chokes, triggers, butts, and the like—pale in importance compared to the fit of the gun. If you have a gun that fits and shoots where you look, stick with it for now.

Gauge

You can shoot any gauge you choose, twelve or smaller. At any shoot, save for a national championship, you probably could shoot a ten-gauge, too, because most of the people gunning that day would risk losing to you just for the thrill of watching your teeth fall out under the recoil of fifty or so rounds from a ten-gauge.

A twelve-gauge, however, is the gun of choice. Twelve-gauge shells loaded with one and an eighth ounces of lead, the maximum allowed by sporting clays rules, are readily available, whereas one ounce of lead is the norm for smaller gauges. That extra eighth ounce equates to more pellets, and pellets are what break clay. Simple as that.

For fun, however, a sixteen- or a twenty-gauge can't be beat. Some women shoot twenty-gauges in competition because of the twenty's lighter recoil. And I wouldn't shoot against them for anything more than a Snickers and a Coke. In the next few years we'll see categories open in all the major events for the small gauges. If you want to get on the bandwagon early, forget a twelve and stick to a twenty. If you are put off by misses, however, you may want to go with the large gauge for now.

Weight

A little weight in a sporting clays gun is a good thing. Weight smooths out your swing and diminishes perceived recoil. Walking from one shooting station to another doesn't give you the aerobic workout of chasing grouse across a New England hillside or following long-legged pointers around a ten-thousand-acre Texas pasture, so weight in a sporting clays gun doesn't penalize you physically.

I recently heard that an English gunmaker has worked out a precise formula for determining the optimum weight of a shotgun, based on the shot charge. By his reckoning, one hundred times the weight of shot (in ounces), divided by sixteen, equals the ideal gun weight in pounds. For example, a sporting clays gun shooting a one-and-one-eighth-ounce load should weigh about seven pounds, which sounds pretty good to me. A field gun shooting a one-ounce load should weigh in at around six pounds. Okay.

I wonder, however, when I hear of such formulas, how they are derived. Skeptic that I am, I'm tempted to think that some enterprising gunmaker built a fine gun for field shooting, weighed it, found it to tip the scales at six pounds, then worked the math backward, using the weight of the gun and the standard one-ounce load, to come up with the magical factor of one hundred.

If you want to experiment with changing the weight or balance of your gun, try adding self-adhesive lead tape or lead plumber's wool (from your local plumbing supply store), which may be stuffed into small cavities in the fore-end or the stock. See the section on recoil in this chapter for other tips.

Barrel Length

The first time I shot sporting clays I used a field grade Fox side-by-side with twenty-five-inch barrels. A quick gun. Too quick. I could bust the targets at the flushing grouse station—doubles through the trees, quartering toward me—where the shot was tight and fast and no farther than fifteen yards, but at a wood-pigeon station, where the shots were all passing at an altitude that looked as if it might require FAA clearance, I shot a week and a half behind the clays. One of my problems was twenty-five-inch barrels; the gun was too short to swing smoothly.

The trend in barrel length today in sporting clays guns is from twenty-eight- to thirty-inch barrels. Some of the hot competitive shooters are even reaching out beyond the thirty-inch length, but twenty-eight inches is a good length for most of us. There is enough forward weight to smooth out your swing without the gun feeling overly awkward. One big factor in selecting barrel length is your physical size. A six-foot-six gunner can easily handle thirty-inch barrels. A five-foot shooter may be overwhelmed by twenty-eight-inch tubes.

Barrel length in sporting clays guns appears to be destined to become one of those faddish variables that changes each year, like the length of hemlines. Don't feel obligated to buy another set of barrels because you've read that the latest hotshot just switched to thirty-four-inch tubes. Try several barrel lengths before you buy, and choose the length that feels most comfortable. Remember, barrel length does not affect choke, pattern, or how far you can shoot—unless, of course, you can only hit things resting on the end of your muzzle.

Rib and Beads

The rib, that strip of metal sitting on top of the barrels, serves as the launching pad from which to propel your vision down the length of the gun and onto the target. The rib is not a sight, per se, but an aid. The width of the rib is a matter of choice. British and European shooters tend to favor wider ribs than Americans. There are arguments for and against the various widths, but none make much sense to me, since you're supposed to be looking at the target and not the rib in the first place. Pick the width that is least distracting.

The rib may have one or two sight beads. Again, this is a matter of personal preference. The alignment of the front and back bead can take on greater importance if the gun doesn't fit properly, for the two beads can then serve as visual references to head and barrel alignment. But if your gun fits and shoots where you look, beads are far less important.

The rib should be matted (slightly stippled) to minimize light reflection. It may also be vented to dissipate heat from the barrel. Some guns are even vented between the barrels to disperse heat and cut down on wind resistance as the barrels swing on a crossing shot. Or so the theory goes. The only time I've noticed wind resist-

The choice between a narrow sight rib (bottom) and a wider rib (top) is a matter of preference. Note the difference in front beads on these guns. The lower gun has a more traditional brass bead; the upper gun has a larger bright white bead.

Some gunners prefer two beads, which can be useful aids in alignment if the gun doesn't fit properly. A well-fitted gun, however, should point exactly where the gunner looks.

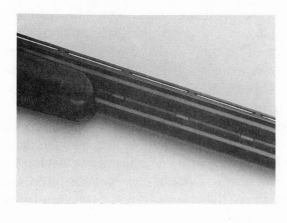

This Browning sporting clays gun features a ventilated rib and ventilated barrels.

ance on a shotgun was when I was twelve and shot crows from the bed of a pickup cruising back roads at thirty miles an hour.

Fore-end

Over-and-under shotguns come with either beavertail fore-ends or finer, more tapered field fore-ends. Converted skeet and trap shooters favor the former; bird hunters favor the latter. Again, it's a matter of taste.

Grip

Most over-and-unders—and all those designed specifically for sporting clays—have pistol grips. Most automatics and pumps also have pistol grips, or semipistol grips. The alternative is a straight English grip, most often found on side-by-side field guns.

Field shooters argue that a straight grip more closely aligns the hands on the same plane, thereby enhancing the pointability of the gun. The control of the gun is more in the forward hand than in the hand on the grip. On a gun with double triggers, a straight grip is also preferred, because it enables the hand gripping the wrist of the gun to slide back a smidge as the trigger finger moves back to the left barrel trigger. A straight grip also trims weight off the gun.

This thinking doesn't carry over into the accepted design theories of sporting clays guns, where pistol grips are favored. One reason for this is that on an over-and-under, the forward hand sits lower beneath the barrel than it does on a side-by-side, because the fore-end on an over-and-under is much deeper than the slim splinter fore-end on a side-by-side. On the over-and-under, therefore, a pistol grip aligns the hands more effectively than a straight, lean wrist. Also, a pistol grip transfers a bit more control to the rear hand, which many shooters feel results in a smoother swing on longer shots. This is more important in shooting targets than birds, because targets usually fly in relatively straight paths, whereas birds

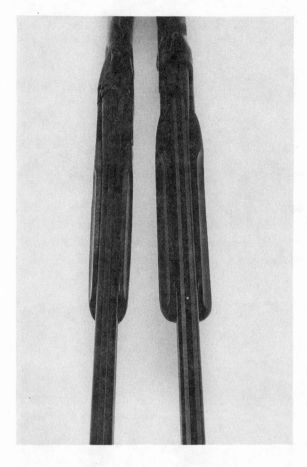

Left, a trim fore-end, often found on field guns. The fore-end on the right is bulkier. The one you select is a matter of personal preference.

tend to dart and dip and vary their flight patterns. With more control in the forward hand, the bird hunter can more quickly compensate for these deviations in flight. The target shooter, however, doesn't need to compensate as quickly. For him, a smooth swing is more valuable, and a smooth swing is more easily obtained when control is more balanced between the two hands.

Since most sporting clays guns have a single trigger, movement of the trigger hand is neither necessary nor desirable. As long as the

31

A pistol grip, preferred by most sporting clays shooters, provides a firm grip and good control for the rear hand. Note that the shooter's head isn't canted over the stock.

On an over-and-under, a pistol grip lowers the rear hand. Because of the greater depth of the fore-end, however, the shooter's two hands are nearly aligned.

pistol grip isn't exaggerated into a bulbous palm swell, like the grip on a trap gun, either a pistol or straight grip will work. But on longer shots, the pistol grip will usually shine.

Safety

No safety catch is a substitute for careful gun handling. Never trust a safety. Never believe that a gun is harmless because the safety is on. Safeties can fail. They do fail. But more often than not, shooters fail—fail to remember that a loaded gun has the potential to do terrible damage.

Double-barreled guns have two types of safeties: automatic and manual. Automatic safeties engage, rendering the gun "safe," whenever the action is broken and then closed. Manual safeties must be engaged by the shooter. Lots of hunters prefer manual safeties because they don't like to leave a job as important as making a gun "safe" up to some unseen collection of springs, ratchets, and cogs in the bowels of the action.

Hard-core sporting clays shooters like a manual safety, too, because they don't want to risk the chance of a safety inadvertently being on when they're in the butt shooting. In practice, many sporting clays shooters take their safeties off before calling for the first pair of targets from a station and leave their safeties off through the last pair tossed. In effect, they don't use safeties at all when they're on the line.

I don't like that kind of thinking. I like to see a safety on whenever the gun is off the shooter's shoulder, as it must be before a sporting clays target flies. I get nervous when I see a shooter thumb off the safety before he calls for a target. It's a bad habit that anyone who ever—EVER—plans to shoot birds should avoid. For a field gunner, thumbing off the safety should be an integral part of mounting the gun.

On many over-and-unders, the tang-mounted safety also serves as a barrel selector. By moving the safety laterally, the shooter can select between the two barrels. In theory, this gives the shooter an opportunity to choose between chokes when a bird gets up. In practice, I've met few shooters who, in the heat of a flush, have the presence of mind to make such a decision and then execute a deft thumb swipe while simultaneously mounting the gun and disengaging the safety. On a sporting clays course, whether or not to use such a maneuver becomes a moot point. The gunner knows which barrel he'll shoot first because he's watched the flight of the birds presented to the shooter in front of him, or, if he's the first shooter, he's asked the trapper for a pair of view targets—birds tossed but not shot.

The barrel selector, then, becomes something best ignored when the time to shoot approaches. Some safety/barrel selectors, however, have a disconcerting habit of sliding laterally as the safety is thumbed off, jamming somewhere between the over and under barrel positions. When this happens, the safety won't slide forward all the way, and the gun won't fire. Practice wiping the safety off with your thumb as you mount the gun without changing the barrel selection or jamming the safety somewhere in no-man's-land.

Trigger

Some shooters like a wide, heavily checkered trigger; others like a narrow, smooth trigger. Some like a rough trigger in the winter when they shoot with gloves and a smooth trigger in the summer when they shoot barehanded. To satisfy those demands, some dedicated sporting clays guns have interchangeable triggers. Turn an Allen screw and off comes one trigger, on goes another.

The length of pull can also be varied on some guns by moving the trigger forward and backward. Such an adjustment can be of some use in fitting a gun to a shooter, although altering the stock length is a more precise and effective method. Changing the length of pull at the trigger is handier, however, for accommodating minor changes in gun fit for the shooter who guns in winter with four layers of clothing and in summer with just a T-shirt.

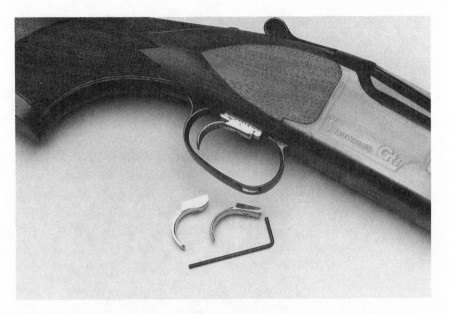

The Browning GTI comes with three different triggers. Replacement involves no more than loosening a set screw.

Butt Pad

One of the rules that defines sporting clays is the requirement that the gun not be mounted until the shooter sees the target. Until that time, the entire butt of the gun must be visible beneath the shooter's armpit. That means, of course, that the gun must make the long journey from a low position to the shoulder. This trip probably accounts for more missed birds than any other aspect of the game. To smooth out a long, often bumpy trip, most sporting clays shooters favor a relatively smooth butt pad with a rounded heel, which is less apt to catch on clothing than the fat, sticky, sharp-edged pad often found on trap and skeet guns. A trap or skeet shooter, who calls for a bird with his gun mounted, doesn't want that gun stock to move one millimeter. But a sporting clays shooter can't afford to have his gun hang on the mount. A near perfect butt pad for sport-

A rounded heel prevents the gun from hanging up on clothing during the mount. The butt on the left is covered with leather; the one on the right is rubber with a radiused heel.

ing clays is a smooth, rounded leather-covered pad like those installed by the Orvis gunsmiths. A quick alternative involves a judicious sanding of the heel of the butt, followed by several coats of nail polish over the newly rounded section.

Recoil

All shotguns have it. A seven-and-a-half-pound twelve-gauge firing a two-and-three-quarters-inch shell with one and an eighth ounces of shot over two and three-quarter dram equivalent of powder generates nineteen foot-pounds of recoil. Recoil doesn't mean much to the bird shooter. In the heat of a flush, most hunters are unaware of recoil, although some notice it the next day when a purple bruise spreads across their arm and shoulder from those six shots they fired before their gun was properly mounted.

If you have no bones to pick with Newton's third law of motion—that bit about actions having equal and opposite reactions—you'll realize there is little we can do to diminish recoil. There are things we can do, however, to minimize kick, which is the best way to describe our perception of recoil.

And for sporting clays shooters, who fire at a hundred or more targets a day, kick deserves some attention, especially since kick on the first shot at a pair of targets can so debilitate a shooter that his second shot is no more than a hail and farewell and some change in the pockets of a shell company.

The gun you choose can affect the way you perceive recoil. Generally, an automatic will kick less than a double. A gun with a straight stock—less drop at heel and comb—will kick straight back at the shoulder. A gun with considerable drop will kick with an upward blast to the cheek. These are things to be aware of, but certainly not sufficient reasons alone to buy a particular style of gun.

Kick can be lessened in several ways. First, try lighter loads. Simple enough: less action, less opposite reaction. You might be surprised how less flinch—our reaction to kick—will improve your scores, even though the effectiveness of the shell is diminished.

Second, if you're shooting a field gun, try adding some weight. Self-adhesive lead tape, which golfers use to change the heft of their clubs, offers an easy way to experiment. Tape it to the bottom of the barrels or cram it in a hole drilled in the stock. The location of the weight will affect the balance of the gun, so experiment before doing anything permanent.

Third, consider having a gunsmith lengthen the forcing cones, the tapered section of the barrel just forward of the chamber that

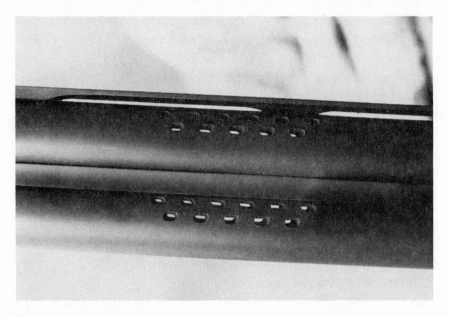

Porting the barrels directs escaping gasses upward, minimizing perceived recoil and stabilizing the muzzle after the first shot.

serves as an area of transition for the movement of shot from the shell through the barrel. You might also consider backboring your gun or having the barrels ported. Backboring increases the overall diameter of the barrel, from the forcing cone to the start of the choke. Porting entails drilling a series of holes in the barrel near the muzzle. These holes allow gas to escape upward, reducing perceived recoil and muzzle jump. Discuss these options with a gunsmith who has solid shotgun experience. And please, don't port Uncle Henry's Purdey.

Fourth, wear better ear protection. Part of your flinch—your perception of recoil—is in response to noise. Cut down the noise, and you'll swear you've cut back on kick.

There are other options, too: recoil reducers that fit in the stock, pads that fit on your shoulder, hypnosis, surgical implants, who knows what else. But try these simple solutions before getting too radical.

Choke

The subject of chokes is a convoluted mess, mired in arcane language, dripping with mystery and misconception. Take the term *improved modified.* Any choke modifies—that is, changes—the pattern. How is someone to know that a modified choke sits about halfway between a full choke and no choke at all, and that an improved modified sits between modified and full? You well might infer from the word *improved* that an improved choke is superior to a modified choke, which leads to the conclusion that a full choke must be the best of all.

Perfectly simple.

Choke is the relative constriction in the barrel of the shotgun from the bore to the muzzle. Not all shotguns of the same gauge have the same bore diameter. Some are overbored; some are underbored. This is why an absolute measurement of the barrel at the muzzle has little meaning. A gun with a muzzle diameter of 0.705 inches may have more constriction—in relationship to the diameter of the bore—than a shotgun with a muzzle diameter of 0.695.

See how simple this is?

Choke is reflected not only in the relative constriction of the barrel but also in the density of pellets thrown on a patterning board at a prescribed distance. If there are any standards in this choke business, they are the parameters defining the patterning test. To perform this test to quantitatively determine choke, tack up a big piece of paper and step off forty yards. Shoot at the middle of the paper. Now draw a circle thirty inches in diameter around the center of the pattern. Count all the shot within that circle. Divide that total by the total number of shot in the shell and express the answer as a percentage. Now consult table 1.

Table 1. Determining Choke

CHOKE	PERCENTAGE from Patterning Test	RELATIVE CONSTRICTION (In Thousandths of an Inch)
Full	70–80	40
Improved Modified	65–70	30
Modified	55–65	20
Improved Cylinder	45–55	10
Cylinder	45 and less	0

Skeet 1 choke, with five thousandths of an inch constriction, falls between cylinder and improved cylinder. Skeet 2, another refinement in the choke game, offers five thousandths more constriction than improved cylinder. These two designations represent such minor changes in choke that computing average percentage of shot thrown is impossible. Their effect on pattern will vary minutely from gun to gun.

If you enjoy shooting paper and counting pellets, you can have a lot of fun with all this. I don't even like to look up how many number-nine pellets are in an ounce-and-an-eighth load, much less count them (okay, I'll do it: 693, give or take a few). So all this talk may have little practical application for you, particularly since there are some other mysterious factors that influence patterns. What counts is breaking clay—or dropping birds—so the pragmatist should forget all the charts and tallies of pellets and see how his choke performs at shooting distances (which rarely extend more than forty yards). He should try a variety of chokes, first on paper and then on clay. He should try each choke with different shells. For example, hard shot in a shot cup will produce a tighter pattern for a given choke than soft shot pushed by a fiber wad.

For a gunner shooting a fixed-choke gun—one without interchangeable choke tubes—the choke of choice for sporting clays is improved cylinder for a single-barreled gun and skeet and improved cylinder for a double-barreled gun (some might argue skeet for both barrels). If your gun has more choke than that, consider having a smith open up the tubes.

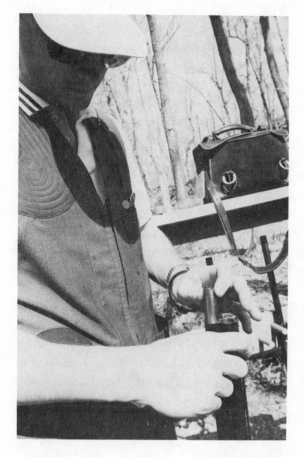

Changing choke tubes. Under USSCA rules, chokes or guns may be changed only between shooting fields, a shooting field consisting of one or more shooting stations serviced by the same trap. At most courses, a field and a station are synonymous.

If your gun has interchangeable choke tubes, as do most sporting clays guns today, you should be perfectly happy with a pair of cylinder chokes or a pair of skeet chokes, an improved cylinder and perhaps a modified. Rarely, if ever, will a target be thrown that demands improved modified, and a full choke is unnecessary.

An even smaller kit might consist of one improved cylinder. That can give you two choke combinations.

Bad math, you think. No, because your gun, without any choke tubes, yields an interesting choke combination dubbed thread and thread.

Gun manufacturers don't recommend shooting a gun without tubes, but I know one exceptional sporting clays shot who has run at least twenty-five hundred rounds through his gun—sans tubes—with no damage. He's careful to shoot only loads with shot cups, and before inserting a choke tube, he carefully cleans any plastic out of the threads with a bore brush lubed with oil. The threads are still sharp and the tubes screw in easily. He claims his thread and thread choking throws the finest pattern you've ever seen.

If there is one bit of advice on chokes that all the best shooters echo time and again it's this: don't get hung up on chokes and blame each miss on the wrong tube. If you are confident in your choke, your shooting will improve—most often from that confidence, less often from that choke. The fabled English shooter A. J. Smith claims his chokes have been rusted in for some time.

Remember also that the USSCA rules of sporting clays stipulate that you may change chokes only between *fields,* a field being one or more stations shooting at targets thrown from the same trap. That can mean you may need to select a choke that is a compromise between several different constrictions. The odds say to err on the side of openness. And remember that you can change the pattern thrown from one choke by changing shells.

SHELLS
◆

Fortunately, the rules of sporting clays limit shell selection some-what: shot size may be no larger than seven and a half; the shot charge may be no greater than one and one eighth ounce; the powder charge may be no greater than three and one quarter dram equivalent. USSCA rules call for "normal production shot." The

NSCA further qualifies that by stipulating that the shot must be spherical, thereby eliminating spreader loads (flattened pellets that open up the pattern).

The rules on reloads are in flux. Currently, the NSCA permits reloads; the USSCA prohibits their use at state, regional, and national championships and at selection shoots. As more shooters take up the sport and discover how many shells they can burn up in a year, such rules may well change.

Truth is, almost any target load with one and an eighth ounces of shot may perform exceedingly well in your gun (I'm talking about twelve-gauge guns here, since a twelve-gauge is most popular and most effective. Shooters choosing smaller gauges must usually be content with one-ounce loads). I hedge a bit and say may, because your gun's preferred diet is an individual thing. There is still some magic left in the world of shells (and chokes). Two guns of the same model with sequential serial numbers and identical chokes may throw different patterns with identical loads. It's best not to ask why; some mystery in life is a good thing.

The secret to selecting the proper load for your gun is simple. The first step is based on economics: find out which brand of shells are most readily available in your area at a reasonable price. Look for two-and-three-quarter-inch target loads by a manufacturer you recognize. You'll want one and an eighth ounces of shot and between two and three quarters and three and one quarter dram equivalent of powder. Select number-eight shot, since that's the size you'll most often shoot. If you value your shoulder, start off with a powder charge on the lighter side. Some sporting clays shooters using light loads—two-and-a-half-inch shells with two and a half dram equivalent of powder and one and one-sixteenth ounces of shot—are finding that the reduced recoil more than compensates for the reduction in powder and shot. What good is more shot downrange if you're flinching so badly that you're three feet off the target every time?

Next, buy a variety of available loads. Select different brands,

Light English loads: two-and-a-half-inch shells carrying one and one-sixteenth ounces of shot over two and a half dram equivalent of powder. Such loads produce less recoil without sacrificing much wallop.

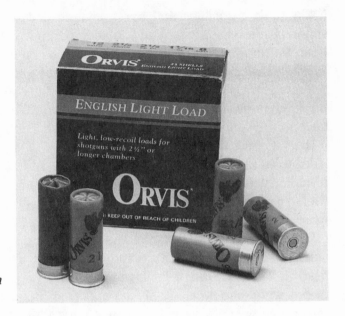

different shot and powder charges, and different shot sizes. Tack up a big sheet of paper, step back twenty-five yards, and pattern each shell with the choke you most often shoot, probably cylinder or skeet. Compare the results. The shell that throws the most even pattern wins. Simple enough.

Now stick with that shell throughout all your shooting until you get to know its strengths and weaknesses. Learn how it performs at fifteen yards and at forty. If you find something about it that displeases you, go back to your patterning paper and pick the next best load.

You may want to take this experiment one step further and pattern for other variables: different shot size, different chokes, different distances. Good for you. Most of us, however, rarely go beyond that initial patterning shot, if we make it at all. I, for one, tend to shoot whatever shells I stumble on—a case of promo loads from the local K-mart, three boxes squirreled away in a closet for ten years, six unmarked loads that have rattled around the pockets of an old shooting vest for an undetermined length of time. That's not the right way to do things, I know, but how can you pass up shells at three dollars a box, and what can you do with those found rounds—have them bronzed?

Shot selection adds an interesting variable to sporting clays. The guiding principles to shot selection are:

♦ The smaller the shot, the more pellets; the more pellets, the denser the pattern.

♦ The larger the shot, the heavier the pellets; the heavier the pellets, the more kinetic energy they store, which enables them to break targets at a greater distance.

♦ The harder the shot, the less it deforms in the barrel; the less it deforms, the tighter the pattern. Conversely, soft shot, particularly soft shot loaded without a shot cup, will deform enough to open up a pattern.

Commercial target loads are available in shot sizes seven and a half, eight, eight and a half (from Winchester), and nine. Eights are the most popular for sporting clays. Most shooters, however, also carry some nines for close stuff and some seven and a halfs for more distant shots. I've spoken with several good competitive shooters who prefer to vary shot size rather than change chokes—something to think about and test on a piece of paper.

One of the newer sporting clays loads on the market is Orvis's Duo-Shot. This shell packs its one-and-an-eighth-ounce pellet load with eights and nines. The theory behind the shell is that the eights will carry well beyond the thirty-five-yard mark, while the nines will fill in the pattern at lesser ranges.

The lesson to be learned from all this is that nothing in the world of guns is sacrosanct. Give different shells a try. See how they work for you. Carry some nine-shot promo loads—those K-mart specials—for tight shots. The soft lead will open the pattern somewhat. And carry some hard shot seven and a halfs for longer targets.

Besides, is there anything more fun than arguing with a friend

Orvis's new Duo-Shot: one and one-eighth ounces of mixed eight and nine shot. The eights carry farther than the nines, while the nines fill in the pattern at close range.

over something that inflames such passion yet has very little significance in the grand scheme of things?

"Hard shot!"

"No cup!"

"Eights!"

"Nines!"

"Okay, wise guy, a six-pack on the next fifty."

"You're on!"

3

Necessities

◆

Moderation is a fatal thing. Nothing
succeeds like excess.
—Oscar Wilde

I lied. You do need more than a
gun and shells. Anytime you shoot sporting clays—almost anytime
you shoot anything, anywhere—you should wear eye and ear protection.

(I don't wear ear protection hunting, I'll admit. Walking through
a grouse covert with wads of insulation in my ears is a cruel form
of sensory deprivation, like making love with gloves on. Besides, the
hunter fires relatively few shells in a day. Sitting on a dove stool
knocking back RCs and running through three boxes to bag a limit,
I'll plug my ears, but otherwise I enjoy the sounds around me too
much to wad up.

I do wear tinted glasses hunting, however, and I've found that
they've improved my shooting. Initially, I wanted to protect my eyes
from the thorns and whipping branches I encounter in Vermont
grouse country. I've had too many weeping eyes from near misses.
After a while, however, I found that good glasses actually helped me

see grouse and woodcock better. They can help you see clay birds better, too.)

On every sporting clays course I've seen or heard about, eye and ear protection are mandatory. Sporting clays is no noisier than other shooting games, but the potential for eye damage is inherently greater. Incoming birds simulating driven pheasant or decoying ducks are always presented, and those birds are often taken directly overhead or just off the shooter's nose. Even a half-decent hit on such targets will spray the shooter—and the spectators—with shards of clay. Shots fired in trees can send pellets ricocheting back at you. And despite the nearly universal use of shooting cages, which limit the arc of a gunner's swing, the occasional overzealous shooter will stretch beyond the restraints and send a charge of shot toward another butt. Course designers try to avoid such situations, but someone inevitably manages to rain shot down on fellow shooters and spectators, even on the most conservative layouts.

You need eye protection—no ifs, ands, or buts. And if you like to hear, as most of us do, ear protection is also a must.

EYES

If you wear glasses, you're set. Most prescription lenses today are made of optical-grade plastic, which is lighter and affords greater eye protection than glass. The only drawback to standard prescription glasses is the way they sit on your face. Most ride too low. With a gun mounted, a shooter often finds his vision partially obscured by the top of the frame. The solution is to get a pair of prescription shooting glasses.

Gunners who wear contact lenses or who have perfect vision (a pox upon you!) have a variety of shooting glasses from which to choose. There are several things they should look for.

First, choose glasses with either optical-quality plastic lenses (CR-39, in the shade trade) or slightly less expensive polycarbonate

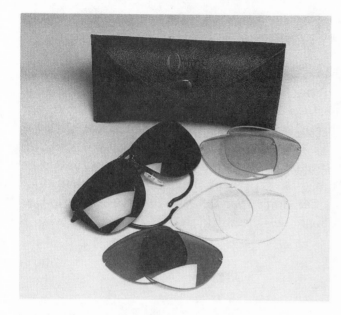

Shooting glasses are a necessary safety item and a great aid to improving your shooting. These glasses have interchangeable lenses in clear, vermilion, yellow, and neutral tints to suit any light condition.

lenses in its better grades. Glass is too heavy and is likely to shatter when struck by a wayward pellet.

Second, select glasses that ride moderately high on your face. Try mounting your gun while wearing them. If you also plan to use them for hunting, make sure they don't ride up so high that a wait-a-minute vine could whip up under the lens and scratch your eye. You need protection from below in glasses for the field. Silicone nose pads are nice, too. They prevent the glasses from slipping when the heat's on and the sweat is pouring down your beak.

Third, choose a lens that filters out some or all of the blue wave-lengths of light. Light in the blue spectrum doesn't focus at the same point as light of other colors. Therefore, sharpness will increase if blue is blocked from your eye. Yellow lenses cut down substantially on blue light.

Fourth, wear the lightest colored lenses that are comfortable. Dark lenses, which can block out 80 percent or more of the ambient light, cause your pupils to dilate. When this happens, perceived visual acuity diminishes slightly, just as depth of field diminishes in a camera when the lens is opened up.

Finally, consider glasses with interchangeable lenses. Different colors, such as yellow and vermilion, can alter contrast, depending on the condition of the light, the background color, and the color of the target. Against a green background, a target often stands out best when seen through vermilion lenses. Clear lenses are nice on those days when the light level is low. Although yellow lenses appear to increase brightness, they cut down light transmission to your eyes by as much as 30 percent, depending on the density of the tint. Just remember, don't wear yellow in one eye and vermilion in the other; you might see the world in 4-D!

EARS
◆

A twelve-gauge shotgun generates about 140 decibels of roar. A chainsaw only puts out 100. If someone hired you to shoot a round of sporting clays, he'd violate OSHA regulations if he didn't provide hearing protection.

The noise OSHA wants screened from your ears is produced by shock waves passing through the air and down your auditory canal. But there's another kind of noise that shooters face, called bone conduction noise. The report of a gun can set the bones in your skull to vibrating like a tuning fork. Those vibrations, producing a sound about twenty decibels lower than that transmitted through the air, auger into your ear, too. A shooter who cares about his hearing must contend with both types of auditory assault.

Three kinds of hearing protection are readily available: foam ear plugs, ear valves, and earmuffs. Each is better than nothing; some are better than others. All come with an EPA noise reduction rating (NRR), a measurement of their efficiency expressed in the decibels of noise they screen out. These ratings are a bit misleading for shooting sports, for they are based on the effectiveness of the devices in attenuating constant environmental noise—the steady

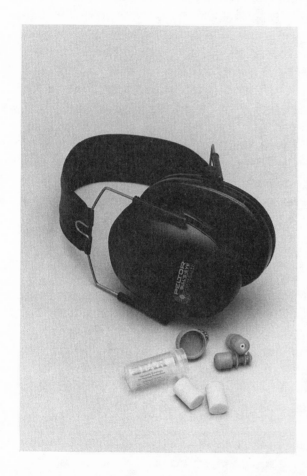

Hearing protection is mandatory, if you like to hear. The muffs (top) are most effective in blocking bone conduction noise. The inexpensive foam plugs (bottom) may be worn with the muffs. The plugs in the center have small valves that screen out loud noises but allow low steady sounds, such as conversation, to pass. The valve opening is visible in the end of the plugs.

hum of a factory machine or the roar of a chainsaw. The ratings don't measure the effectiveness of the plugs or muffs in screening impulse noise like the blast of a shotgun. Keep that in mind. This inconsistency in testing is the reason that the decibel-level rating on valves is so low; they're designed to permit the wearer to hear steady background noise, such as conversation, and to screen out impulse noise.

Foam ear plugs that fit any ear, short of Mr. Spock's, block out a lot of noise—thirty to thirty-five decibels' worth. They're cheap and relatively easy to use. Most shooters I know cart four or five pairs in their vests, shooting bags, and pockets. Roll them into little pills and pop them in your ears, and they'll expand to fit quite snugly.

Plugs have three drawbacks: they don't block out bone conduction noise; they do block out normal conversation, including jeers, encouragement, and cries of "LOOK OUT!" as the anchor bolts to the high tower pull out and sixty feet of structural steel start a fast descent toward your head; and they feel like a pair of mice have set up housekeeping in your skull.

Ear valves are rubber or silicone plugs with discriminating valves that transmit normal conversation yet block out loud noises. Well-fitting valves should screen about the same impulse noise as foam plugs (although their NRR ratings won't reflect this). Valves do nothing for bone conduction noise, but they do permit normal conversation. They are the protection of choice, certainly, for the hunter afield.

Earmuffs cut out up to thirty decibels, and they dampen bone conduction noise. If they have a drawback for sporting clays, it is that the bulkier muffs, which are often the best, can interfere with gun mounting. Some shooters adjust; others never feel comfortable in muffs. The only sure-fire test is to try out a pair. Orvis has a special shotgunner's muff that is specifically designed not to interfere with gun mounting. They carry an NRR of twenty-one, which is pretty good.

Many shooters opt for both plugs or valves *and* muffs. A combination is, by far, the best protection, especially if a shooter is wearing glasses, as he should, because the glasses' temple pieces partially break the seal of the muffs.

ADDITIONAL GEAR
◆

With your eyes and ears protected, you're ready to shoot. You really need nothing else, save for a gun and some shells. However, a few accessories can make a round of sporting clays more enjoyable. Last year I attended the USSCA National Championship in Kansas City to see what went on at the top level of competition. On the day before the start of the contest, a course was open to competitors for a practice round. The rest of the world—we hackers—could shoot, too, so my friend Ted Hatfield, a gunmaker from St. Joseph, Missouri, who had a booth at the shoot, and I decided to give the course a whirl.

I'd brought glasses and hearing protection to wear during the competition, so I was covered there. Ted grabbed one of his nifty little side-by-side twenty-gauges, we bought scorecards and eight boxes of shells, and headed off to the course.

Have you ever tried to walk while carting two hundred shotgun shells in your pockets? You can't. Ted finally found a plastic shopping bag in his car. We hauled shells through three stations in that sack. Finally it blew out, scattering a hundred rounds of eights down a hill in front of a teal station, thereby stopping all shooting at that butt while we retrieved our *cartuchos,* as Ted likes to call them. Although we were shooting pretty well for two rubes using the same gun (the barrels of which got so hot that the second man to shoot at each station had to wrap his hand in a handkerchief), we looked like stumblebum stunt men for a John Candy film.

The point is, you need a few accessories to make the game more pleasurable—and less buffoonish. The first item on the list is an adequate shooting vest. A vest serves several purposes: it provides plenty of pockets for shells, chokes, a handkerchief, glasses, and such, and it endows the gunner with a clean sweep of leather or fabric from his shoulder to his waist. This is quite important, for that smooth, unencumbered surface prevents the gun from catching on a pocket or a fold of fabric when it's mounted. That patch also serves as a firm base on which to shoulder the gun. Gun mount is all-important in this game. A floppy shirt or a rough sweater can be enough to obstruct a clean, smooth mount. A good shooting vest takes care of that problem handily.

An option—or an adjunct—to a vest is a shooting belt, an ex-

Vests are handy for carrying all the paraphernalia a sporting clays shooter acquires. The smooth leather patch on the shooting shoulder of a vest insures a clean gun mount, too.

panded version of the shell pouch skeet and trap shooters wear. A good belt offers a few extra pockets to hold choke tubes, some heavier shot for distant targets, a pair of gloves, perhaps, and hearing protection. Such a belt is particularly nice in hot weather (a shooting shirt with some padding in the shoulder will keep the fabric from bunching up as you mount your gun). Orvis has such a belt made of leather that would also work well in a dove field. The longest pouch would hold a couple of Cokes right handy.

You can't load a vest with a hundred shells, however, which is what you need for a big shoot (plus a box of nines for the close stuff and some seven and a halfs for the birds that make you reach). Some sort of bag—other than a plastic grocery sack—is useful for toting shells, water, a small towel to mop your brow, and this book.

This Orvis shooting belt offers a convenient place to carry chokes, shells, gloves, hearing protection, glasses, and a Coke or two.

A well-made leather case is ideal for carrying the shells a gunner needs for a round of sporting clays. Left, a clamshell doctor's bag. Right, a more conventional design.

Three types of choke changers. The two larger units have been adapted from power screwdrivers; the small unit is a manual speed choke changer.

There are several models available, from elegant clamshell doctor's bags to more traditional shell cases.

Anyone who gets beyond the first three rounds of sporting clays will fall victim to choke juggling. Selecting the proper choke for any one station is important, certainly, but early in your sporting clays career, choke selection takes on near-mystical proportions. "I know I could have cleaned all ten (instead of three) if only I'd shot four-thousandths more choke in the top barrel."

Sure.

I've seen shooters agonize for thirty minutes over which choke to use, while ten other shooters cleaned all ten at that station with fixed chokes ranging from skeet and skeet to modified and full. The proper chokes can make a substantial difference, but having confidence in what you're shooting can mean even more.

The one thing you don't want to put up with is a lot of needless juggling of tubes and wrenches when you do change chokes, so a choke carrier, which straps on your belt and holds your chokes in some logical order, and a speed changer, for screwing the things in and out, are brilliant accessories.

Speed changers come in two guises: fast and faster. The fast ones are manual jobs that look like something a plumber might use. The faster ones are battery-driven cousins of power screwdrivers. And many a nineteen-dollar electric screwdriver has been turned into a choke tool with a little imagination and a wad of glue.

Finally, there are those accessories that make a round of sporting clays just a bit more enjoyable. Gloves are one. Some shooters feel a pair of thin, tight gloves gives them a better grip on the gun, and thereby greater control. Others just like the feel of leather on wood. I, for one, like to shoot with a glove on just my left hand. I hunt that way, using the glove to fend off puckerbrush, so I feel more comfortable gloved. Fortunately, no one has mistaken me for Michael Jackson.

Yet.

There are other, more esoteric, accessories out there waiting for you. The ubiquitous shoe protector—a small flap of leather that

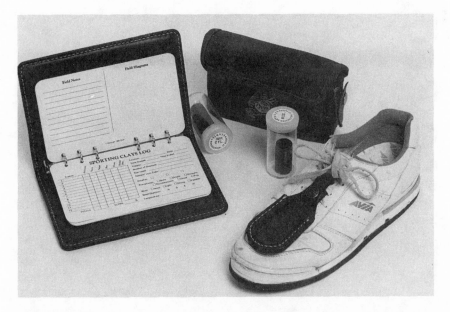

Handy accessories. From top, clockwise: a choke carrier with extra chokes; a shoe protector; a sporting clays logbook in a leather binder.

laces onto your shoe—has crossed ranks from the trap range to the sporting clays field. This device is intended to protect the top of your Reeboks when you rest the carbon-encrusted muzzle of your gun on the toe of your shoe. Without this protection, your favorite sneaks look like a midget stubbed out his cigar on your foot. Why people like to rest a gun on their toe is beyond me; it's not a particularly safe habit for a hunter to acquire. You don't want to do it if you're shooting a pump or an automatic. With a break-action gun, such a posture is all right when the gun is broken; in fact, with a break-action gun, resting the muzzle on your toe is one of the more comfortable poses you can assume while waiting to shoot. (With its action broken, a double doesn't sit well in a rack, nor does it rest easily in hand with its butt on the ground.)

There are sporting clays shoes out too, with dark toepieces to

These shoes, designed expressly for shooting, have a heel wedge, which pitches the gunner's weight slightly forward, and a protective toepiece on which a shooter may rest the muzzle of his gun.

conceal those unsightly carbon rings and slight heel lifts to pitch you forward a bit on the balls of your feet, like a good prizefighter setting up a jab. You don't want to shoot off your heels. If you can't distribute your weight on your own, these shotgunning elevators might help.

One of the nicest small accessories I've seen is a simple leather-bound notebook in which you can record the pertinent details of each round of clays. You may not want to remember the score, but it's fun to look back and see with whom you shot, the weather of the day, and who had to pay for beers at the end of the shoot.

Finally, there are racks upon racks of tweedy clothing, which has found much favor among Anglophilic shooters. It's good-looking stuff, for sure. If you can wear it well, without looking like a Monty

Python parody of the ugly American, be my guest. But don't think tweeds are obligatory for shooting a round of sporting clays. Granted, *Town and Country* has done a spread on an ever-so-posh shoot, where everyone wore a tie and, when not shooting, assumed a slightly bored posture, one hand holding up a broken over-and-under and the other holding down a Range Rover. A lovely shoot. But you don't need that stuff.

Sneaks and jeans and your old hunting vest will work just fine. Now that you're ready, let's see what the enemy looks like.

4

Targets, Traps, and Courses

◆

You are now my enemy, and I am yours.
—BENJAMIN FRANKLIN,
on shooting his first
round of sporting clays

In the last few chapters we've talked about the things that are on your side in this game. Now we must face the enemies: the target, the trap, and the course on which you shoot.

TARGETS
◆

Modern clay pigeons are made of asphalt pitch and ground limestone. The pitch is heated to 350 or 400 degrees and mixed with the limestone in varying proportions, depending on the target being built. The mixture is cast into molds and cooled, much like a huge batch of candy.

On a sporting clays range, you may be presented with as many as eight different types of targets (three of which are variations on the same theme). The rules stipulate that in a competition, 64 percent of the targets thrown must be standards. In practice, it's rare

60

that even 30 percent of the birds will be those devilish deviants, the nonstandard variety. Usually it's more like 15 percent.

Nevertheless, the oddball targets are fun. They add spice to the game. In the case of the rabbit and the battue, they create shots that wouldn't exist otherwise. Let's call the roll.

Standards

There are three minor variations of the standard clay pigeon, all of which turn up on sporting clays courses from time to time. The stock-in-trade, skeet-trap-backyard pigeon is the one with which we are most familiar. It measures 108 mm in diameter and comes in assorted colors, like Life Savers. A few clay pigeon manufacturers further subdivide this category into a consumer division, molding a pigeon with less pitch (the binding agent) and more limestone

A selection of sporting clays targets. From top, clockwise: rabbits, midis, minis, battues. In the middle: standard sporting clays targets (108 mm).

(the filler). These pigeons are more fragile than their commercial kin. White Flyer, the General Motors . . . no, bigger than that, the Sony of clay target manufacturers, doesn't differentiate between skeet, trap, and consumer pigeons. When you buy AA White Flyers at Monty's Sports, you're getting the same bird that flies at skeet and trap ranges.

The next step up in this standard breed is a sporting clays pigeon, which is the same size as the skeet-trap bird, 108 mm, but which is beefed up a bit to withstand faster velocities. Consequently, the sporting clays standard pigeon is slightly heavier than its plebeian relatives.

The third variation is the international standard, 2 mm wider and five grams heavier than the sporting clays bird. Many sporting clays courses used international birds in the early days of the game because *standard* standards blew apart too often when thrown at high velocities. You'll still see an international from time to time.

It's very important to recognize that there are three distinct varieties of standard targets. Should you ever miss a bird in the standard family, throw your hat on the ground, break your gun, and storm off, yelling at the top of your lungs, "Bloody hell, that was an international bird! If I'd known you sots were throwing such stuff, I'd have come prepared for it, but you just spring it on me while I'm standing on the line like a bloody fool, expecting a bloody hundred and eight millimeter target!" Such a tantrum will impress everyone around you and cause many spectators to forget that you have never broken more than twenty-two birds out of a hundred in your life.

White Flyer offers its sporting clays standards with black or orange domes. Other manufacturers also paint birds white. In truth, there are no perceptible differences between the subspecies.

Midis

Midis are the transvestites of sporting clays targets: they'll fool you at a distance. A midi measures 90 mm in diameter, doesn't have the dimples of the standard (the dimples stabilize the bird in flight, much like the dimples on a golf ball), and is about 2 mm shorter. Midis are either all black or all orange.

Midis are the most popular of the specialty targets. When thrown as part of a pair with a standard target, a midi looks like a standard that is farther away and faster. Midis come off a trap at a higher speed than a standard, but they don't carry as far. A pair of midis is particularly deceptive. Even an experienced sporting clays shooter will often mistake such a combination for a pair of standards flying ten or fifteen yards farther out.

Here's a secret for distinguishing midis from standards: ask the trap operator.

Minis

If you're over thirty-five, you may recall the MO-SKEET-O trap and target, a small pigeon-tosser in the shape of a pistol that was designed to clamp on the barrel of a smoothbore .22. The trap threw a miniature clay pigeon that was just about impossible to hit. Some of us were taught wingshooting with the MO-SKEET-O; it probably set us back three or four years.

A mini is about the same size, 60 mm in diameter. Minis are all black. They are affectionately known as flying aspirin. That should tell you something.

A mini is very fast out of the trap, yet quick to fade. Because it has less mass than a standard or a midi, it expends its energy quickly. That characteristic is the key to hitting them. Give a mini some time to get out there, and it will slow down and almost die. Almost.

Minis come only in basic black, which makes them nearly impossible to see against a dark background. They aren't particularly difficult to break, however, so nines are often the shot of choice.

The one great advantage of a mini is that the target is so small that should you miss, you can claim that the pigeon found a hole in your pattern. A lot of people will believe you. And sometimes a mini *will* find a hole.

Battues

A battue, pronounced "bat-two," has the same diameter as a standard but only 30 percent of its height. A battue looks like the pancakes we used to eat in the army. But softer.

Known affectionately as flying razor blades, battues lack the dome and dimples of standards and therefore have little, if any, aerodynamic stability. They fly erratically, dipping and diving in the slightest breeze. As they lose speed, they tend to peel off in one direction or another, which is often the best time to shoot them. Their profile is so slim that they can be impossible to see—or hit—until they do lose speed and bank into a dive.

Battues are often thrown as pairs, one bird stacked on top of another. This opens the option of tossing four battues at once; the gunner then must try for two. Covey shooters, of course, go for all of the birds at once and fail to hit any.

Battues are black—of color and of heart. Probably the most humbling target presented to a sporting clays shooter is a pair of battues thrown in an erratic wind.

Rabbits

Rabbits are the same diameter as battues and standards and about the thickness of two battues. Rabbits have thick rims, and instead of a dome on top, they have a depression—and so will you, after encountering a few. Rabbits are designed to take the abuse that comes from being bounced across the grass. They come in black and white.

Of all the clay targets, rabbits are the least predictable. Even a battue can be counted on to peel off at the end of its flight, but a rabbit always has a surprise up its paw.

Rabbits will take lead and not break. I've seen a rabbit with seven pellet holes in it. The target wasn't awarded to the shooter because no visible break could be seen by the judge.

A rabbit is thrown by a trap with its arm mounted in a vertical plane. The target is pitched underhand, like a bowling ball, not overhand, as in a game of crocket—or is it cricket? I've also heard that rabbit targets can be presented by simply rolling a rabbit down a relatively steep chute. Such a launch would be perfect for a home course, particularly when combined with a trap-thrown bird in a fur and feather presentation.

Rabbits are not as fast as they look. In fact, they are the slowest of all targets because of the friction they encounter when they hit

A two-armed trap for throwing a rabbit and an aerial target at a fur and feather station. The top arm throws the bird; the side arm, which swings along a vertical plane, throws the rabbit. The rabbit arm has just been triggered.

the ground. They are challenging, however, because they can vary their path vertically, by bouncing up in the air, as well as horizontally. Most rabbits are taken relatively close and succumb quite nicely to number-nine shot, although I've heard of a diabolical rabbit target shot across a pond at forty-five yards. The man who told me about this shot said he had to hold so far in front of the target that he had time to break his gun and lower it before his shot connected with the clay. Rabbits make you tell that sort of tale.

Specialty Targets

The rules of sporting clays don't prohibit the use of any oddball target that may come along; in fact, a challenge is always encouraged. "Any sporting clays target approved by shoot officials" is the NSCA wording; appended to that is a nod of approval to a thing called a ZZ-Pigeon, which, I understand, has propellers and requires a special trap for launching. No sane person of my acquaintance has ever seen one.

There are, however, a couple of other specialty targets that crop up from time to time. Rockets are squat standards. They have no perceptible dome and more mass in the middle; consequently, they die a bit faster than standards once they begin to lose velocity. Rockets are quite rare.

Exploding targets, often seen in Starshot, that televised shooting match that's a combination of a video game and a celebrity show, break up into satisfying puffs of powder when hit; otherwise they fly like standards. Exploding targets are all for show, so you'll rarely see one on a sporting clays course.

Quite soon we'll see more biodegradable targets (White Flyer has some out now). They'll be a boon for the backyard course, where the litter of pigeon parts is enough to discourage frequent shooting.

The last category of clay pigeon is not a particular type but rather a designation imposed by the course official. I'm talking about a poison or hen bird, a pigeon of a certain color declared by whoever is running the shoot as a protected sex or species.

If black and orange pigeons are the colors of choice in targets for a particular station, a white pigeon may be designated as a hen. You cannot shoot at a hen. If you shoot at and hit the hen, you'll be scored a miss; if you shoot at and miss the hen, you'll be scored a miss; if you don't shoot at the hen, you'll be scored a hit. Poison birds are never thrown as simultaneous pairs. I have seen a poison bird thrown with a legal standard, however. The presentation was such that the two birds crossed in front of the shooter and above him. The only things visible until ten yards before the birds crashed into the trees were the undersides of both. The undersides, of course, were black. Therefore, the shooter couldn't fire until the last moment for risk of blasting the poison bird.

◆

A final word: don't be intimidated by any one type of bird. They all break. If you don't believe that, buy a selection and stomp on one of each in the garage. It's good to establish the vulnerability of your enemy.

TRAPS
◆

Unless you plan to open your own sporting clays course, the type of trap that flings birds for you is of little importance. Raw speed and distance are not the principal factors in target presentation. This is a game of deception, of obstruction, of subtlety, of psychological warfare. Targets should be presented to approximate the flight characteristics of game birds, and no game bird I know of flies at eighty miles an hour. Shots should be within ethical hunting range, too, so targets that require sky-busting at eighty-five yards should not be thrown.

Still, the characteristics of traps have some effect on the way the game is played. Here's a look at the major types.

67

The ubiquitous Trius trap, the mainstay of backyard clays.

Consumer Traps

The ubiquitous Trius trap, sold in every Wal-Mart, every sporting goods store in the country, is one of those marvels of American engineering that hasn't changed in twenty years or more. I have one Trius that is fifteen years old and two others that are three months old, and I can't see any difference between them.

Trius traps are great for backyard courses; some are probably in use at commercial shoots. They have only three drawbacks. First, they don't throw a particularly flat target; that is, their power is such that clays lob out on a parabolic course. Second, they aren't made to stand up to the punishment meted out at a sporting clays course, shot after shot, day after day. Third, they have only one arm, so doubles must either be stacked or placed on the arm one behind the other. This causes the birds to come off the trap at different angles.

Manual Traps

Sporting clays courses should be dynamic, changing layouts every so often to keep shooters entertained and challenged. Manual traps, which mount on the simplest of stands and which require no electricity, provide that flexibility.

Manuals are hand-cocked, hand-loaded, and usually hand-operated traps that are built with strong bearings and industrial-strength parts to stand up to the rigors of commercial shooting operations.

They can throw a variety of birds without breakage. With some modification, they can throw rabbits. Their elevation can be adjusted so they can throw targets straight up in the air for springing teal stations. They usually have dual arms so two targets can be tossed on parallel paths, like a fighter pilot and his wing man, not with one going left and one going right, as happens when two targets are placed one behind the other on the same arm.

Quality manual traps throw flat targets at long ranges, so they can present incoming birds tossed from a distant position or crossing birds thrown from well out of the range of the gun. This ability to throw a target from afar means the pigeons come in silently, on cat's feet, so to speak (a prize here for the worst cross-species metaphor of the year). The gunner isn't alerted by the clank of a nearby trap. Most traps at sporting clays ranges fall into this category.

There are two kinds of manual traps: full-cock traps, which must

A manual trap in operation at the 1989 USSCA National Championship. The trapper should have been wearing eye protection, even though he sat behind a protective berm.

be cocked by pulling the arm back through the full arc of their swing; and three-quarter-cock traps, which employ a clutch that enables them to be cocked by rotating the arm through a quarter revolution. The latter are preferred by sporting clays ranges for their ease of operation. They also insure that when throwing a following pair or a report pair from one trap, the second bird can be airborne a little sooner than a similar bird thrown from a full-cock trap.

A trapper manning his station. The plywood protects him from stray shot. He'll don glasses and hearing protection when the shooting starts.

Automatic Traps

Automatic traps are high-ticket jobs that are only found at commercial shooting operations. Many are skeet traps that have taken on a new role. Some are designed specifically for sporting clays, including wobble traps, which can oscillate at random on two axes. Although an automatic trap may appear to have many advantages, their high maintenance requirements, initial cost, and limited portability have made them less than desirable in the eyes of many range operators. The one exception may be at high towers, where automatic traps obviate the need for a trapper to climb up and down.

◆

Should you have an opportunity to operate a trap, be careful. They can be dangerous. You don't need to offer one of your favorite

A trapper throwing a view target for a straight-away flush shot. The gunners are visible behind the brush pile to the rear of the trap.

limbs as a new type of target. Never reach across a cocked trap to pick up a pigeon. Never trigger a trap when anyone is standing on the side of the throwing arm. Use common sense.

If you are in the market for a trap (or traps) for a backyard course or a commercial operation, consider these questions:

- Is the supplier going to be around in five years when you need a part?
- Is the trap versatile: able to throw parallel pairs (from two arms), rabbits, teal?
- Is the bearing in the trap—the part most subject to wear—a quality part? Ask who makes the bearing.
- Are the trap components of solid quality?
- Is the trap easy to maintain?

◆ Is the trap new to the market or has it been around a while and stood the test of time?

Last I looked there were a dozen or more manual traps being peddled to sporting clays operations. Not all will survive the cut, so buy wisely. A small savings today may become a big machine shop bill tomorrow when some widget breaks and you find the company has abandoned its line of traps for electric cork-pullers.

COURSES

Where you shoot is a function of where you live. Sporting clays courses are sprouting up around the country—at skeet and trap ranges, at shooting preserves, at hotel/resort complexes, in back-yards. The NSCA and the USSCA, whose addresses are on page 177, will send you listings of member courses. Most courses affiliate with one group or the other.

Some courses are elaborate affairs with thirty or more stations and such a mind-boggling array of target combinations that the owners must strain madly to come up with a suitable sporting name for each station (most of which are in the nominal league of surf and turf). Others are more modest. I've heard of a course in Massa-chusetts set on three acres with two traps. Fourteen shooting sta-tions revolve around this setup, with twenty-five targets in all.

A course layout is a function of the imagination of the designer and the talents of those who shoot there. Obviously, one doesn't set up a course that would send world-class shooters into apoplexy if the average-Joe member is still working on his first case of shells. On a sporting clays course, par should be in the neighborhood of 50 percent. (Par should mean average; in golf it has come to stand for extraordinary performance.) An adequate shot—not a begin-ner, not a member of the club team, but an average, decent shot—should break twenty-five out of fifty targets.

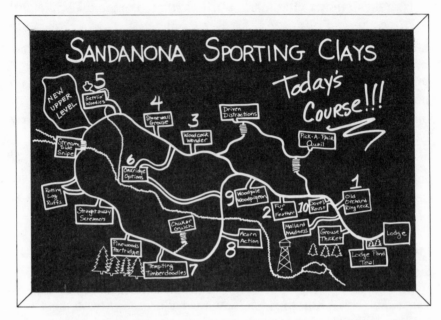

Out of twenty available shooting stations on its lower field, Sandanona selects ten for the course on any given day.

Sporting clays ranges are run on a membership basis or are open to the public, or both. Some are open all the time; others, usually smaller courses, are open just on weekends or by appointment. Many sporting clays operations love to put on special events—corporate shoots, private parties, even wedding receptions—and the better ones will tailor the course to the ability of the shooters, striving for that 50-percent par.

What's a good course, from the viewpoint of the shooter? One that challenges you the first time and the twentieth. One that changes periodically. One that is efficiently run. One that welcomes guests and spouses. One that provides instruction and solid lessons in safe gun handling to new shooters—or ill-taught old hands.

I've seen several courses with two shooting stations per field, one presenting the birds to the gunner at more of an angle than the other or with less of a window through which to shoot. This setup is analogous to the men's and women's tees on a golf hole. A handicap is built into each station, so shooters of various abilities can sport about together without holding back or embarrassing anyone.

Some courses are elaborate affairs with massive towers (one course in South Carolina has a fire tower from which to launch birds). Others are elegantly landscaped and boast sumptuous club-houses. Those things are secondary. Flexibility and ingenuity are the keys. A bare-bones course with four or five single manual traps and a scattering of hay bales to protect the trapper may offer the best shooting. Don't be overwhelmed by amenities. The shooting is what counts.

Don Valentine, a friend of mine who is an exceptional shot and who has gunned all over the world with the likes of A. J. Smith and the great English instructor, Jack Mitchell, tells me that some of the best sporting clays courses he has shot in England are no more than temporary setups. "An instructor will haul three or four traps to a farmer's field, set up a few shooting cages, protect the trapper with hay bales, and there you have it: instant course," says Don. The beauty of this system is that the setup takes maximum advantage of terrain. Nothing is static. The course is always changing.

On the other hand, some of the grand courses I've seen in America are far too elaborate to tear down and rearrange each month. They have become as static as golf courses, where course dynamics are measured by how often the cup is moved on the green. That's a disadvantage for the gunner. Birds don't follow predictable flight patterns; courses shouldn't either.

As a final note, pay attention to the safely rules. If the club doesn't require that spectators and shooters wear eye and ear protection at all times while on the range, get the rules changed. And if you see a potentially dangerous situation, such as a shot on which an unchecked wide swing might throw lead on another station, call the range manager quickly and stop shooting until the problem is corrected.

Safety first.

5

Basic Wingshooting

◆

When you have to think,
it's already too late.
—ANONYMOUS

Shooting things out of the air is a complex activity; the more we talk about it, the more we analyze it, the more complex it becomes. Unfortunately, the more complex it becomes, the more we feel we must think about it, and the more we think about it, the less successful we are at busting feathers or clay.

Imagine Joe Montana going through the mental gymnastics some wingshooters perform. He'd need a front line that could sustain a protective pocket for an entire quarter and receivers anchored with cinder blocks to keep them in range while he factored distance, position of defensive players, wind, speed of receiver, and the effect of the earth's rotational force.

But Joe doesn't do any of that. He picks his man and throws, relying on hand-eye coordination to send the ball deftly spiraling to the outstretched fingers of his receiver. Most of the time it works. Just ask any Broncos fan.

Shooting things out of the air is no different. We can't compute;

we have to rely on our innate hand-eye coordination and the ability of our brains to factor all the variables for us instantaneously. We see the target and point at it with our shotgun. We don't aim. We don't calculate. We look, point, and shoot.

Perhaps the finest aerial shooter I've ever seen is a Methodist minister in his late sixties named Stacy Groscup. Stacy puts on shooting demonstrations all over the country. Dressed in buck-skins, he shoots foam discs, clay pigeons, and, for his finale, Bayer aspirin out of the air.

And he does it all with a bow and arrow.

An arrow is about the same diameter as an aspirin, so there is little room for error. An open choke doesn't factor in here; you could backbore a bow until the cows came home, and the pattern wouldn't open up one bit.

How does he do it? Simple. He doesn't aim. He simply trusts his computer, which, as he likes to say, he wears between his ears, and he relies on his inherent hand-eye coordination to line things up. He concentrates on the target, watches it closely in flight, moves his hands together in a synchronized motion, pointing at the aspirin with his lead hand and drawing back the bow with his right. When he hits his anchor—the point where the bow is at full draw and his right hand is against his jaw, analogous to the point at which a shotgun is fully mounted and the stock cheeked—he fires. Look, point, shoot. Splat—aspirin annihilation.

If a senior-citizen Methodist minister can do that, we should be able to whack clay pigeons with a shotgun, shouldn't we?

THE EYES HAVE IT
◆

Hand-eye coordination should be called eyes-hands coordination, for the eyes are the first element to come into play—both eyes. The eyes lead, the hands follow. Unfortunately, for some of us the eyes lead us astray. Just as 30 percent of the world is left-handed, a

Determining eye dominance. If you bring the cardboard up quickly, it will frame your dominant eye.

portion of the world is left-eyed. Their master eye—the one that lines things up—is their left eye. This would work out quite nicely if all left-handed people were left-eyed and right-handed people were right-eyed, but that's not always the case. Some right-handers have a dominant, or master, left eye. Conversely, some left-handers have dominant right eyes. It is imperative that the wingshooter determine eye dominance before doing anything else; otherwise the finest-fitting gun and the most diligent practice will be for naught.

Determining eye dominance is straightforward. Take a piece of cardboard a foot square and cut a two-inch hole in the middle. Hold the cardboard in both hands at waist level. Select a target on a distant wall—a mark, a picture—and stare at it intensely. Quickly raise the cardboard in front of your face so the target is centered in the hole. Now shut your right eye. If the target is no longer visible in the hole, you have a right master eye; if the target is still visible, you have a left master eye.

If that confuses you, or if the target jumps around as you shut your eye, simply bring the cardboard back toward your face, keeping the target centered in the hole. Keep coming until you frame one eye with the hole. That eye is your master eye.

If you are right-handed and have a right master eye or if you are left-handed and have a left master eye, shooting things out of the air will be relatively easy (some of the time). If, however, your eye and hand dominance are at odds, you must address the problem before you do anything else.

For some reason, more women have this cross-dominance problem than men, so women should pay particular attention to testing for eye dominance. In addition, a few people have a weak master eye. In such cases, the nondominant eye may assume dominance some of the time. Don't despair; there are solutions.

The simplest is to change the side on which you shoot. If you're right-handed and have tried to shoot from your right shoulder but you have a left master eye, learn to shoot from your left shoulder. It's not as difficult as you may think. Practice mounting the gun every day for a week, then try shooting some clays off your left shoulder. It will feel awkward at first, and you'll need to put some effort into mastering the mechanics, but when you start hitting pigeons, you'll realize that switching shoulders was well worth your while.

If you're a new shooter, switching shoulders will be less difficult.

That's why it's important to establish eye dominance early in the game.

If switching shoulders is an insurmountable obstacle, or if you have a weak master eye—right dominant most of the time but occasionally switching to left dominance when you mount the gun—try shutting your left eye (if you shoot from your right shoulder) just as you mount the gun. Some shooters can get away with merely squinting their left eye. It's important to remember not to shut your eye before the gun is mounted, because you then loose your binocular vision, which helps your brain compute the speed and distance of the target, and you cut down on your peripheral vision, which enables you to pick up targets quickly as they enter your field of vision.

If shutting an eye is awkward—and some people simply cannot shut just one eye—experiment with placing a small piece of tape on the left lens of your shooting glasses so it blots out the middle of the vision of your left eye (again, we're assuming a left master eye for a right-handed gunner). In his classic book *Shotgunning, the Art and the Science,* Bob Brister suggests cheeking the gun and, with the fore-end supported by a friend, dabbing the index finger of your lead hand in a bit of Vaseline and smearing it on the left lens of your shooting glasses. This works particularly well for people who have a weak master eye and a tendency for the eyes to switch dominance. The Vaseline obscures the left eye image, so the right eye maintains its dominance without blocking peripheral vision. And since the blurry spot on the glasses is determined when the head is firmly cheeked to the stock, the view is barely obstructed when the head is upright, before the gun is mounted.

If all else fails, you can have your gun fitted with a crossover stock—wood with a severe dogleg—which keeps the gun mounted on the right shoulder while aligning the barrels with the left eye. Crossover stocks are hard to fit and less than perfect, however, so they should be considered as a last resort. They look like hell, too.

Most cross-dominant shooters can solve their problem by mounting the gun on the shoulder of their master eye or by shutting one eye or patching their glasses.

◆

Once eye dominance is established, the shooter needs only to let his innate abilities take over. To see how easy this is, look at that target on the wall again. Now point at it.

Very good. I've yet to meet a person who couldn't point. Try it again. If your finger had been loaded with an ounce of eights, you'd have blown away that picture of Aunt Matilda. We possess an amazing ability to look at something and align our finger with it without aiming, without calculating. This talent enables us to hurl a snowball, hit a tennis ball, even smack a baseball traveling at eighty-five miles an hour—on a curve, no less. Sometimes we whiff, of course, but the very fact that we can connect a fair portion of the time is a strong argument for the intrinsic accuracy of hand-eye coordination.

THE MYSTERY OF LEAD
◆

But I'm not shooting at a stationary target on the wall, you say. I'm shooting at a moving object hurtling through the woods from left to right at forty miles an hour. The laws of physics say that you can't point a shotgun at a crossing target and expect the shot to intercept it. If shot traveled at the speed of light, perhaps it would break the pigeon, but shot doesn't go that fast. By the time the shot arrives at the place where you pointed, the target will be gone.

You're right. You must shoot in front of the target, you must give it forward allowance, you must lead it, which means all this talk about pointing and shooting must be hocus pocus. . . .

It's not. Really. Remember Montana. His receivers run from left to right, too. Lead is part of his game. Let's look at the accepted ways shotgunners tackle lead and see how you can make hand-eye coordination do most of the work.

There are four schools of thought on hitting a moving target: spot shooting; sustained lead; swing through; and instinctive shooting (or the Churchill Method). All four can work, do work. Some lend themselves more readily to certain shooting situations than others.

Spot Shooting

This method involves pointing the gun at a precise point in front of the target and firing before the target reaches that point, so that shot and target arrive simultaneously. Spot shooting works for some skeet shooters, because the flight path of each bird is very predictable. An experienced shooter knows that if he aims his gun at a specific point and fires when the bird reaches another predetermined point, shot and bird will collide. To determine those points requires a lot of practice and very consistent targets. Spot shooting rarely works for live birds or sporting clays targets, where inconsistency is the rule of the day.

Sustained Lead

Fans of sustained lead track a target with the gun held a specific distance in front of it. Waterfowl shooters are traditional practitioners of sustained lead. "I was four duck lengths ahead of that mallard," is a comment heard frequently around blinds. Sustained lead can work, but it takes a good bit of practice and exposure to targets flying at similar speeds. Sustained lead also demands a certain amount of calculation. In pass shooting, an experienced gunner can pull it off, but in upland shooting—and in sporting clays—there are too many variables at work and too little time for most of us.

Swing Through

Also called pass through shooting, swing through requires less conscious effort. Swing through is often used effectively by sporting clays shooters. The shooter tracks the target on its line of flight, pulls through it, and fires as the muzzle of the gun passes the bird or, on more distant shots, pulls slightly ahead. Swing through demands a smooth swing and steady follow-through. If the gunner stops his gun as he fires, the result, predictably, is a miss.

Swing through works, but it also has two weaknesses. First, the gunner can turn swing through into sustained lead by sweeping through the bird and then trying to adjust his lead, the distance he sees between the end of his muzzle and the target. He does this, most often, because his eyes shift from the target to his gun. He sees a certain gap, does some fast computation, believes he is too far ahead or too far behind, adjusts, and misses. Second, swing through is a conscious movement—the shooter is fully aware of target and gun as he tracks the bird and wipes it out with the muzzle. Should his concentration falter during the shot—as it often does—his eyes tend to shift to the gun and he stops pointing and starts aiming. Instead of taking advantage of his natural ability to point, he segues into a more intellectual mode. When he panics in his calculations, the gun jerks to a halt and the bird keeps on flying.

Instinctive Shooting

This method—also called the Churchill, modified Churchill, or English method—avoids many of these problems. It's the technique taught at the Orvis school. Instinctive shooting has the great advantage of factoring out all the intellectualizing that goes on in other approaches to wingshooting. It's simple to teach and effective for almost all bird shooting and most sporting clays shots. You'll notice I hedge there; most sporting clays shooters with whom I've discussed wingshooting technique and who practice instinctive shooting admit to modifying their technique on certain shots. Specifically, they often slide into a version of swing through on longer shots and on hard crossing shots at medium distances and beyond.

Nevertheless, they do rely on instinctive shooting as the foundation of their technique and for most of their shots. Instinctive shooting offers quick gratification for the new shooter and a solid foundation on which to expand wingshooting technique.

And it works.

Instinctive shooting involves several steps. First, the shooter visually concentrates on the target from the moment it appears until the instant it disintegrates. He doesn't look at the gun, at the rib, or at the front bead. The more effectively he blots out those pieces, in fact, the better his shooting becomes.

Second, the instinctive shooter tracks the target with his eyes, building in a swing with his body and his gun *before the gun is mounted.* He doesn't bring the gun to his shoulder and then start a swing on the bird. He combines swing and gun mount into one smooth move.

Third, the instinctive shooter points his lead hand (the left, for a right-handed shooter) at the target as the gun is mounted. The left hand sets the pace and points. The right hand helps raise the gun—it doesn't aim the gun. The moment the butt of the gun settles into his shoulder and the stock snuggles against his cheek, he fires. He doesn't calculate a lead; in fact, he shouldn't be aware of the muzzle, other than as a blur in his peripheral vision. He doesn't aim. He focuses all his attention on the target, locked on, so to speak, like radar. But he does keep swinging through the shot. He follows through, for instinctive shooting involves a very fluid movement, not a jerky, hasty point.

This fluidity, in fact, is what builds a lead into each shot—albeit a lead that is not consciously calculated. The shooter picks up the bird with his eyes, building in swing as he mounts his gun, and fires when his gun is mounted—just as the Reverend Stacy Groscup fires when he brings his bow to full draw. The miraculous factor here is that in the time it takes for the brain to send a fire signal to the finger, for the finger to respond, for the trigger to release the sear that drops the hammer and hits the firing pin, for the firing pin to hit the primer, for the primer to ignite the powder, and for the powder to propel the shot on its course, the gun will, in fact, move ahead of the target—will lead it. And the faster the target, the faster the swing of the gun and therefore the farther the lead. This built-in lead is what makes shot and target collide, not complex calculations by the shooter.

The foundations of instinctive shooting are confidence, concentration, and smooth, easy mounting of a gun that fits and that therefore points exactly where you look. Without a well-fitting gun, you must visually align the barrel and the target—you must aim. And without a smooth mount, the gun, which is but an extension of that pointing finger, won't flow smoothly into natural alignment with the target. Let's look, then, at these two important components. Since the majority of shooters are right-handed (and have a dominant right eye), all references are for right-handed gunners. Lefties need simply flop all mentions of right and left, as they are well accustomed to doing.

THE MOUNT
◆

The mount of the gun must come first, for the way a gun fits is directly related to how you hold it and mount it. Without proper stance, swing, and mount, gun fit is a moot point.

The mount begins with your position as you face the target. Most of us have grown up aiming rifles. Thus, when handed a shotgun, most of us assume a rifleman's stance: feet lined up nearly perpendicular to a line running to the target, head cranked over our left shoulder. This is an adequate position for aiming; it's inadequate for pointing.

Try it. Pick a target on the middle of a wall. Assume a rifleman's stance with your left foot pointing to the right corner of the wall, your right foot pointing to the right wall, your torso twisted to the left and your head cranked over your left shoulder. Now point your left index finger.

Awkward, isn't it? Now try this:

Point your left foot at the target. Now position your right foot so the toe is in line with the instep of your left foot. Your right foot should point slightly to your right, in a natural stance. Spread your feet six to ten inches apart—whatever is comfortable, but not too wide. Too wide a stance will cause problems as you swing.

Note that your shoulders are nearly square to the target. Nearly. Your left shoulder should lead just a bit. If you could load a twelve-gauge shell in your belly button, you should be able to hit the target.

Don't lock your knees. Relax. Relaxation is key. But don't scrunch down as if you were a cop in a combat pistol stance. You should look more like a golfer than a tennis player. You're not going to jump laterally. Now bring up your left hand and point at the target. Smoooooothly.

Did you notice that you shifted your weight forward slightly, that you may have nodded your head a bit in the direction of the target? Just a slight tilt forward, not a head-bobbing yes.

Do it again. Raise your left hand and point at the target. Does your finger blot out the target or is it just below it, just a hair? Probably it's slightly lower than the target. That's your natural pointing ability coming to the fore.

Now, without moving your feet, twist your torso and head slightly so you are looking at the left corner of the room. Now bring your eyes back to the target and simultaneously raise your dexterous digit and point at the target.

Right on, right?

That's the basis of instinctive shooting, of the Churchill Method, of the fabled English schools. If we'd listen to it, believe in it, trust it to be the foundation of all our shooting, we'd shoot far better than we do.

You're not going to shoot with your finger, however; you need to get that gun in your hands.

Open the action of the gun to make sure it isn't loaded. This should be a reflex action whenever you pick up a gun. If you have

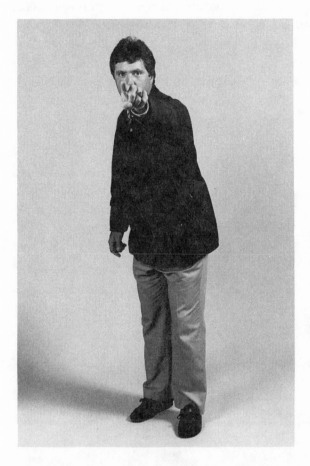

Our natural hand-eye coordination enables us to look at an object, then quickly point at it. Note that the pointing hand lines up slightly below the eye, in the same relative position as the barrel of a gun.

snap-caps, slip them in. If not, load an empty shell (best to keep a couple of empties on hand for dry firing—they cushion the firing pins. Cut the plastic casing in half so there will never be a chance of loading a live shell for indoor practice).

Assume a good stance. Now grasp the gun with your left hand on the fore-end and your right hand at the pistol grip. Don't hold the fore-end back by the hinge pin; that's not a natural extension for your pointing arm. You don't need to assume the straight-arm stance of someone mounting a bayonet charge, but most gunners should run their hand out a bit farther than they do. Many good shooters run their left index finger along the side of the fore-end in a natural pointing gesture.

Close the gun and place the butt under your right arm. The heel should be close to or actually nestling under your armpit. Remem-

The ready position: left foot pointing at the target, gun nearly level, buttstock tucked under the arm, eyes on the target.

ber, in sporting clays the butt must be visible. That's good. With the butt visible you're in a solid ready position for shooting anything that flies. Tuck no more than two inches of stock under your arm. Any more and you'll risk hanging up as you mount the gun.

The end of the muzzle should now be in front of your face but below your eyes so as not to obscure the target. The muzzle should point at the target. The gun should *not* cross your chest at an angle in the high port position many of us were taught to assume when walking up birds. Don't drop the butt of the gun so low or raise the muzzle so high that you look as if you're standing at a sloppy present arms, either. The barrel should be close to level, although the height of the muzzle above the butt may vary, depending on the target. Your lead hand should be close to extended but still have some bend in the elbow. You should be relaxed, comfortable, and alert.

If you don't feel relaxed, comfortable, and alert, something's wrong. Check yourself in a mirror. Videotape yourself. You shouldn't be contorted. Instinctive shooting is predicated on natural ability and requires doing things naturally.

Now is the moment of truth. You're going to point at the target with your left hand, which just happens to be cradling the fore-end of a shotgun. You'll extend your left hand, which will bring the gun forward. Since your right hand is holding onto the gun too, it will follow, like a good dance partner. It won't lead, however; your left hand does that.

As your lead hand comes forward and up, the gun is raised toward your face. Smoooooooooothly. You have more time than you think. A jerky mount will result in a jerky shot. The mount should be all slip and slide, with no hasty, wasted motions. The gun should move up to your face; your face shouldn't be lowered to the gun. As the gun meets the bottom of your cheekbone, your gun shoulder rolls forward slightly, and your head nods into the gun, not laterally (to the side) but forward. *Minimal head movement is all-important in maintaining hand and eye alignment.*

The gun being mounted. Note that the shooter's head doesn't move until the gun is firmly in his shoulder. Then his head tips forward slightly.

The heel of the stock should now be level with the top of your shoulder. The butt should be in the hollow between your deltoid muscle and collarbone, not on your arm.

As the gun is brought up, your weight naturally shifts forward, smoothly, onto your toes, with more weight on your lead or left foot. And when the gun is mounted, fire. Don't start thinking about lead, about the relationship of the muzzle to the barrel, even about hitting the target for now. Simply point at the target and fire.

That's not so hard, is it?

While all this is going on, of course, your radar tracking system—your eyes—have been locked on the target. Not anywhere on the target, mind you, but on the smallest piece of the target you can discern: the head of a bird. The forward edge of a clay pigeon. The *B* in Bayer on that aspirin tablet. Concentrate with your eyes, but don't tense up your body.

Intense eyes, relaxed body.

Bang.

◆

The target on the wall isn't moving; a clay target is. Nevertheless, the sequence of events is the same. All you must do now is follow the target with your eyes and smoothly point at it with your lead hand.

Your eyes track the target; your shoulders and hips follow the target as you pivot on the balls of your feet. As the gun is brought toward your face, it's already swinging. The muzzle, which started out below your eyes, is tracking the bird. Because the gun is nearly level as it's raised, the preliminary swing of the entire gun is built in. The target isn't blocked out. Your eyes are tracking. Your body is pivoting. Point your lead hand at the target, roll your shoulder into the butt, nod your head forward slightly, and fire.

A famous caveat: It ain't over till it's over. This is a dynamic action, and nothing should stop. If you come to a screeching halt when you hear the gun go off, you will have missed. Your lead hand must continue to move, to track. Your eyes must stay riveted on the clay.

Bang.

That's the basis of a good gun mount, whether on a moving bird or a spot on the wall. Instinctive shooting is in us all. You must do it a good deal, however, to develop your natural ability. Don't think this will come instantaneously. Practice is a part of anything. You must train your muscles to respond in certain ways. You must make that gun mount automatic, smooth, unhurried, and clean. You must not shift your focus to the gun. You must not stop.

All this hinges on having a gun that shoots where you point, when you point where you look. Just because your lead hand, which holds the gun by the fore-end, points at the bird, the gun doesn't always shoot in that direction. To exaggerate this concept, grab a yardstick in your left hand and hold the other end of the yardstick— the end analogous to the butt of the shotgun—on the outside of your right shoulder. Now assume a good ready position and point your lead hand at a target on the wall.

Your eye and your hand will be aligned with the target, but the muzzle end of the yardstick will be pointing off to the left. That's an exaggeration of what happens when you shoot a gun that doesn't fit.

GUN FIT
◆

The big question is, how do you know when a gun fits?

The answer is ambiguous, a line the Cheshire cat might purr: The gun fits when the gun mounts smoothly and shoots where you look. However, the gun may shoot where you look and still not fit.

Nothing like a straightforward answer to start off.

The ambiguity lies in the fact that most of us can adapt to standard gun dimensions by contorting our bodies a bit—wrenching our necks over to the side, cranking our shoulders forward, moving our hands. We can hit with such a gun, even though it doesn't fit. We'd hit a lot more frequently, however, if we didn't have to go through those contortions.

The hardest shooters to fit are people new to the sport, who have no idea how to mount a gun, and very experienced gunners, who can readily adapt to almost any stock dimension after mounting the gun a couple of times.

Fit is a function of several basic stock dimensions. Let's look at them and see how they affect shooting.

Length of Pull

You must be able to get the gun to your shoulder without dragging the butt against your clothing and without stretching your lead hand so far that your elbow locks and the gun slips through your grasp. Should the butt of the gun drag, the muzzle may come up before the stock, and the gun will shoot high.

A smooth mount is a function of the length of the stock, which is measured from the trigger to the butt and called the length of pull. The average length of pull for an off-the-shelf shotgun is fourteen to fourteen and a half inches.

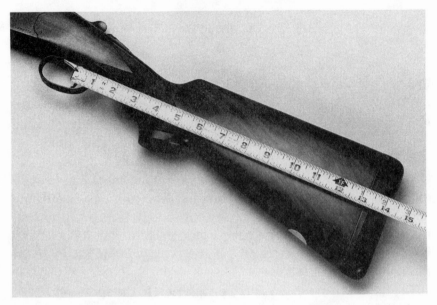

Pull (14¼" here) is measured from the trigger to the center of the butt pad.

Length of pull has some secondary effects on shooting. First, if the length of pull is too long, the gunner will often mount the butt out on his bicep, where, after a few rounds, he will acquire a lovely purple bruise. With the gun butt stuck way out there on his arm, he'll also tend to crossfire. The gun will now look like that yardstick, with its muzzle pointing off to the left. This is particularly noticeable on high, incoming birds: as the shooter reaches up and arches back for the bird directly over his head, his lead hand pulls the muzzle off to the left.

Second, length of pull determines where your cheek touches the stock. Since the stock is rarely parallel to the rib (that is, has the same drop at comb as drop at heel), the position of your face on the stock affects the drop at cheek. A shorter stock may raise your head; a longer stock may lower it.

An overly long stock causes more problems than a stock that's too short, but short-short isn't the answer either. Too short a stock may place your cheek against your thumb, which will jam in your eye on recoil, causing pain and suffering. Too short a stock also has the opposite effect on mounting of too long a stock: the butt comes up ahead of the muzzle, rather than on line with it; when the gun is fully mounted, the muzzle tips down slightly. The shot will be under the target.

Drop

There are three measurements of the distance from the top of the stock to the top of the rib. The first is drop at comb, the distance from the rib to the stock at the comb. Drop at heel is, not surprisingly, the distance from the rib to the stock at the heel of the butt. Drop at cheek, the distance from the rib to the point where the cheek contacts the stock, is less precise, for it can vary on the same gun from shooter to shooter, depending where their cheeks hit. Drop at cheek determines the vertical relationship between eye and gun.

Drops are easy to measure. Place your gun on a flat table with the front bead extending over the edge (if the gun has a middle bead, you'll either have to drill a small hole in the table top for it to nestle in or place the gun on small shims, the height of which will then be subtracted from the overall measurement). Now measure the vertical distance from the table top to the stock at the comb and at the heel. The average drop at comb is about one and a half inches, at heel about two and a half inches, and somewhere between the two at cheek.

Changing drop at comb or drop at heel affects drop at cheek; however, changing both—decreasing the drop at comb while increasing the drop at heel, for example—can change the dimensions of the stock without changing the drop at cheek. Think of the top of the stock from comb to heel as a seesaw pivoting on your cheek, and you'll understand what I mean: one goes

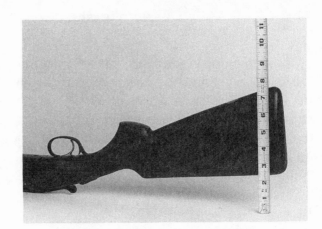

Drop at heel (2¼").

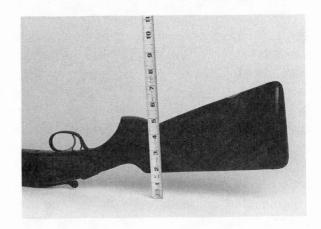

Drop at comb (1¾").

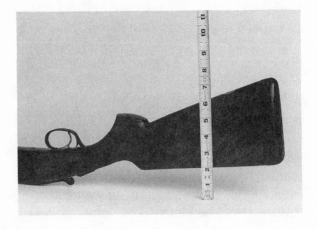

Drop at cheek (2").

up, the other goes down, but the pivot point remains the same.

If a shotgun were a rifle, the rear sight would be the shooter's eye and the drop would be the elevation adjustment. If the drop at cheek is decreased, the shooter's head—the rear sight—is raised. The shooter now sees more rib and the gun shoots higher. Conversely, if the drop is increased, the shooter's head is lowered. The shooter now sees less rib and the gun shoots lower.

This is something of an exaggeration, because no decent shotgun is built with so much or so little drop that your head is cranked up or down like a tang peepsight on a Model 94 lever-action rifle. Variations in drop are minor. The practical effect of changing the drop is to move the shot pattern up and down and to present a view over the rib with which you're comfortable.

Remember when I said that drop at heel and comb can both be changed with no net effect on drop at cheek (and therefore no net effect on elevation)? Why then, you might ask, would you change both those dimensions so that the net change at the cheek is zero?

The reason has to do with perceived recoil. The straighter the stock (the less drop at heel), the more the recoil is directed back into your shoulder. The more bend in the stock (the more drop at heel), the more the recoil is directed into your cheek. A rule of thumb is that the difference between drop at comb and heel should not exceed one inch.

Cast

Cast is a measurement of how much the stock is bent, left or right, off the axis of the barrels, as measured at the butt. Cast comes in two varieties: cast-off and cast-on. Cast-off measures a bend to the right off the axis when the gun is viewed from the top, muzzle facing forward. Cast-on measures a bend to the left of the axis.

Cast-off or on is usually a small increment, a quarter inch or so.

To use the rifle analogy again, cast is the windage adjustment. Because our faces are odd-shaped at best, most of us need a bit of

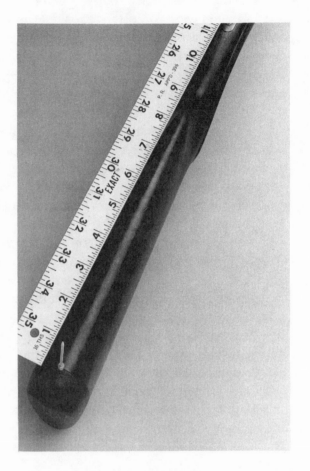

Cast measures the bend of the stock off the axis of the barrel. This stock has cast-off: it's bent to the right for a right-handed shooter. (The ruler is laid along the center line of the barrels. The upright pin marks the center line of the stock. There's a quarter-inch deviation between the two.)

cast to bring our eye into alignment with the rib of the gun and to eliminate the need to roll our heads to the side. A right-handed shooter needs cast-off; a left-handed shooter, cast-on.

Pitch

Pitch is a measurement of the angle formed between the butt of the gun and the barrels. If you place the barrel of your gun vertically against a wall and the butt sits square on the floor, your gun has no

Pitch is the measurement of the angle formed between the butt of the gun and the barrels. This gun has positive pitch. With its barrels against a wall, the toe of the gun is raised slightly off the floor.

pitch (or a pitch of zero degrees). If the toe of the butt is slightly raised off the floor when the barrel is against the wall, your gun has positive pitch (the angle formed between the plane of the barrels and the plane of the butt would be less than ninety degrees). Conversely, if the heel of the butt is off the ground, your gun has negative pitch (the angle formed between the plane of the barrels and the plane of the butt is greater than ninety degrees). Most off-the-shelf guns have about plus four degrees pitch.

Pitch conforms the butt of the gun to the natural contour of your shoulder and chest, making the fit more comfortable and decreasing the perceived recoil. Since most women have more protuberance in that part of their chests than men, a little more pitch in a woman's gun makes shooting more comfortable.

Pitch can change where a gun shoots. Picture a properly mounted gun again. Now envision increasing the pitch by shaving off some wood from the toe. When the butt was seated firmly against your shoulder, the muzzle would drop. The gun would shoot low.

◆

There are other stock dimensions, but they are highly sophisticated, well beyond the scope of this book. Suffice it to say that the custom English shops take into account the thickness and length of the wrist, the cant of the butt, the overall stock thickness, et cetera, et cetera, et cetera.

So be it. The four measurements we've discussed—length of pull, drop, cast, and pitch—are enough to fit most of us. From there on, the law of diminishing returns kicks in. (I've never had a problem finding pants to fit, yet I've never had to reveal on which side I "dress." You can get a gun to fit without getting ridiculous.)

The best way to get a gun to fit—to shoot where you look—is to be fitted by a qualified fitter using a try gun, a shotgun built with an adjustable stock. The fitter will usually take your physical measurements and observe how you mount a gun to come up with preliminary stock dimensions. He'll set the try gun to those dimensions,

Eyeballing the cast in a try gun. The try gun hinges at the wrist, allowing cast-on or cast-off to be dialed in. The shooter then fires the gun at a patterning board. When he sees where the pattern hits, cast can be added or subtracted to alter the point of impact.

have you shoot at a patterning board, make some more adjust-ments, repeat the process as necessary, and finally arrive at a set of stock dimensions that should produce a gun that shoots where you look. That's the way the Orvis school does it, and it works: over the years, thousands of shotgunners have improved their shooting by making a few minor adjustments to their stocks.

You can fiddle a bit yourself, too.

First, consider length of pull. Does the gun mount smoothly, without catching on your clothing? Does your eyeball collide with the back of your hand? Somewhere in between those extremes is a length that is comfortable for you. The rule of thumb is that the gun should come up naturally, without grabbing on anything; once it's mounted, someone should be able to slip a couple of fingers between your cheek and the base of your thumb.

Second, consider drop at cheek (a function of drop at heel or comb, remember). First, try shutting your eyes and mounting the gun. Do this several times to establish a rhythm. Now bring up the gun and open your eyes. What do you see?

No rib at all? You probably have too much drop at cheek.

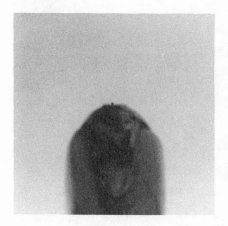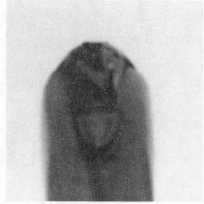

Too much drop at cheek produces a sight picture that shows no rib and well may obscure the front bead.

101

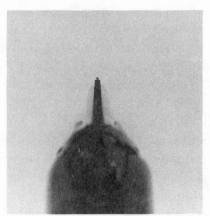

Not enough drop at cheek yields a view that takes in the entire rib.

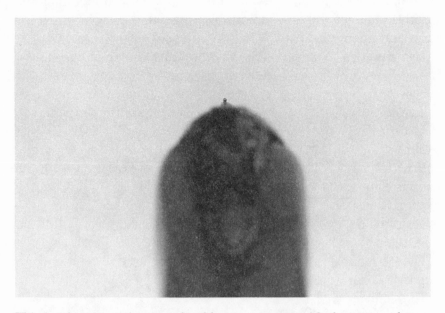

This is what most shooters should see on a gun with the proper drop at cheek.

The whole length of the rib? Not enough drop.

Although individual shooters have varying preferences for how much rib they see, most game and sporting clays shooters like to be able to see the front bead and about a third to two-thirds of the rib. That should put the pattern a third to two-thirds high on a target at twenty yards.

The best test for comb height involves a patterning board. A piece of whitewashed plate steel, which can be repainted after a couple of shots, is ideal, but not all of us have that. Try several sheets of heavy cardboard instead. Draw a bird-sized target on the cardboard, back off twenty yards, load up, assume a good ready position, mount the gun smoothly, keeping your eyes focused on the target, and fire.

Do that a half-dozen times, changing cardboard targets before they're shot out. What you're trying to do is overcome your tendency to aim at the target and let your pointing ability take charge. Ideally, a pattern will develop: the shot will be centered on the target or high or low.

If you're high, you must increase the drop at cheek (effectively lowering your face, your rear sight). If you're low, you should decrease the drop at cheek (effectively raising your rear sight). How much? A smidge, a whisper. As little as a sixteenth of an inch change in drop at cheek can perceptibly move the pattern. Then try it again.

How do you change drop? A temporary measure to decrease drop is to build up the stock with moleskin. A temporary increase in drop is more difficult. One solution is to add a recoil pad or boot to lengthen the pull, which will move your face farther toward the butt, thereby increasing the drop at cheek.

The permanent solution is to remove wood. I've done that on a hundred-dollar pump, but I wouldn't try it on a good gun.

The same test—and the same caveat—holds for fiddling with cast. If you're a right-handed shooter and your patterns hit to the left, you need cast-off. The opposite is true for a lefty. Rarely, if ever, will a

Patterning a gun. The target backstop is whitewashed steel. The gun's pattern is clearly visible.

right-handed shooter pattern to the right or will a left-handed shooter pattern to the left.

You can simulate some cast by dishing out the stock. Sure looks nice. Home remedies for cast—and for other fitting ills—are dicey at best. Better to take your gun to a competent gunsmith, who can measure you with a try gun, arrive at your dimensions, and then bend your stock, build it up, cut it down, lengthen it, shorten it, and do whatever else is needed to make it shoot where you look.

◆

That's not all there is to it. Of course not. If wingshooting were that simple, that easy to master, it wouldn't be any fun. The subject of shooting things out of the air will be debated, discussed, and analyzed as long as one of us still misses from time to time. Of course I haven't missed since 1962, but I heard you still whiff every now and then.

Which brings me to the subject of missing. Don't let a miss get you down. Don't spend time diagnosing failure. Keep your confidence up. Concentrate on the next bird, the one you *will* break, not on the last one that got away.

If you must search for answers, look to the most simple explanations:

- ◆ You stopped your swing.
- ◆ You switched your eyes from the target to the gun.
- ◆ Your mount was too fast.
- ◆ Your gun doesn't fit.
- ◆ You peeked, lifting your head from the gun (and therefore from alignment with your lead hand) when you fired.

Beyond that, let someone else figure out what you did wrong. No one plays golf today without taking a lesson or two. Why not do the same for your shooting? An hour with a qualified instructor will do wonders for your scores. Casual sporting clays shooters—hunters in particular—can benefit immensely from time spent with a pro. None of us shoots enough to develop our potential, to use that muscle memory and instinctive ability to groove our shooting. By the same token, few of us shoot so much that we develop terrible ingrained habits. Bird shooters are, by nature, more flexible in their shooting than target shooters. We can be retrained.

Only the birds will complain.

6

Sporting Clays

♦

Butt, belly, beak, bang!
—British shooting maxim

Your gear is gathered, your shooting style refined. Time to get on with it.

Round up some friends, locate the nearest sporting clays course (contact the USSCA or the NSCA, whose addresses are listed at the end of this book, for listings of their affiliates), and plan on a shoot. Don't enter a competition right off; you'll be intimidated. Plan on a relaxed couple of hours with pals. If you can, schedule an hour-long group lesson with a shooting instructor for the same time.

Before you head out, pattern your gun. You should have done that long ago, but you probably didn't. Now that you have your gear together, spend ten minutes seeing where that gun shoots (after all these years). And take another five minutes to practice mounting your gun from a good ready position. Don't rush. Close your eyes on several mounts, then open them to see how much of the rib is visible. Remember: left hand leads. Gun to the head, not head to the gun. Concentrate on the target.

Chamber two snap-caps, pick out a target on the wall, mount your gun smoothly, and fire as the stock comes to your shoulder and the barrel comes through the bird. Do that a dozen times.

Now you're ready. Gather your gear, grab four boxes of shells, and go.

◆

At most sporting clays courses, you'll sign in at a clubhouse, receive a scorecard, which will help you keep track of your score and help the course owner keep track of how much you've shot, and be

Reviewing course layout with the trapper before a shoot.

turned loose. If several of you are shooting together, you'll want to rotate around the course as a group. You can visit stations in any order that suits your fancy. On a slow day, a trap operator— called a trapper in sporting clays argot—may accompany you. He'll describe each station, if you like, and throw a view pair of birds for the first shooter. On a busy day, trappers may be assigned to each station. Your group will then circulate around the course on its own, and you may have to move in a prescribed order. When you arrive at a new station, you'll call to the trapper for a view pair.

A round of fifty sporting clays will cost you between twelve and thirty dollars; the price depends on the amenities of the course, the land prices in the neighborhood, and what the traffic will bear. To that figure add the cost of shells. A tip for the trapper is nice, too, if the same person pulls all the traps for you.

SAFETY

No matter how long you've handled guns, safety at a sporting clays course should be foremost in your mind. Two rules should guide you.

1. NEVER LOAD YOUR GUN until you are in the cage, the trapper is manning the trap (call "trapper ready?" and wait for his reply), and your gun is pointed downrange.
2. YOUR GUN SHOULD BE BROKEN (or, for an automatic or pump, the action opened) whenever you are not in the shooting cage at a station. The only exception to this rule might occur when you place your gun in a rack. Broken doubles do not stand up well.

If you are a new shooter, heed this advice: get some lessons in shooting and safe gun handling before you chamber your first

*In the butt. The
gunner must not
load his gun until
he's on the line.*

round. You cannot learn safe gun handling from a book. Sporting
clays has attracted many neophyte shooters. That's a good thing;
shooting sports can use them. But I've observed at several courses
that these newcomers, although quite capable shooters, do not
have the ingrained safe gun handling skills of many shooters who
have been around guns all their lives. I qualify that statement a bit,
you'll note, because some people who have grown up with guns are
lax in their gun handling.

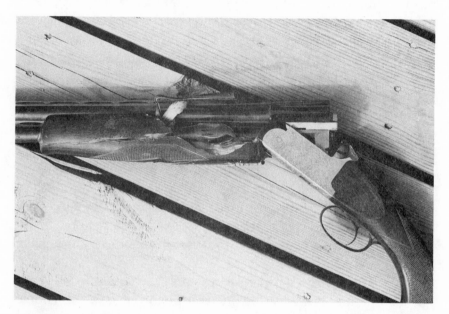

This is what happens when a careless gunner inadvertently slips a twenty-gauge shell in a twelve-gauge gun, then loads a twelve-gauge shell in the chamber and fires. The obstruction has ruptured the barrel and shattered the fore-end. Be extremely careful about separating shells.

In addition, wear ear and eye protection at all times. And if you see something unsafe, call a halt immediately. It's only a game.

Be careful out there.

GETTING DOWN TO SHOOTING
◆

Where to start on the course is usually up to you. Occasionally, you'll visit a sporting clays range on a crowded weekend when so many shooters are on the course that you must slip into a pattern of rotation or risk standing around half the day. Most times, however, you can start at whichever station catches your fancy. Unlike golf, the order in which you shoot is unimportant. Many tournaments are shot in random order, in fact. It's called European rotation. A time limit is set for the shoot, and competitors are handed scorecards. The order in which they complete the course is up to them. The alternative to European rotation is squading, in which shooters are placed in groups that proceed together around the course in a designated order.

Some gunners prefer to attack the more difficult shots first. Others like to warm up with easier targets. With the latter approach, a gunner runs the risk of destroying his confidence for the entire round if he doesn't shoot well on that "easy" first station.

Perhaps the best approach is to view all stations as challenging and none as either easy or hard.

Most courses throw five pairs to a station, ten targets in all. That's not a firm rule, however. Before you head out, ask the course manager to run down all the stations with you. If there are more than you plan to shoot, ask him to select those that he feels might be most appropriate for your ability.

And try to be half honest about that ability.

You'll want to keep score. Not for posterity, perhaps, but to keep track of who's up at any given station and when that person has completed his turn in the cage. Traditionally, a hit is called out as "hit," "killed," or "dead." A hit is a hit when the scorekeeper detects a "visible piece" fractured from the target. A miss is referred to as "lost" or "missed" or "miss."

Mark a hit with an X, a miss with a 0.

Should a target break on launching or fly on a course that deviates substantially from what has been thrown to other shooters at that station, the scorer should call out "No bird." The target(s) should then be rethrown.

If the second pigeon in a pair is the errant or broken bird and the shooter has already shot at the first bird of the pair, two additional birds will be thrown. This is called a proof pair.

A proof pair is thrown to allow the shooter a shot at the second bird without giving him the unfair advantage of having to concentrate on and shoot at only one bird. When the proof pair is thrown, the shooter must shoot at both targets and attempt to hit both targets (you can't fire the first barrel in the air from a ready position). If the shooter fails to fire at the first bird of the proof pair, he'll be scored a miss for the second, whether he hits the second bird or not. (Hitting or not hitting the first bird is immaterial; the score for the first bird of the pair is recorded from the shooter's attempt at the first pair, the attempt on which the second bird was declared a no bird.)

For example, if a shooter misses the first bird in a pair and the second bird breaks coming out of the trap, he will receive a miss for the first target. A proof pair will then be thrown. The shooter must fire at the first bird of the proof pair; whether he hits it or not, his score for the first bird is a miss, taken from his shot at the first pair.

His shot at the second bird of the proof pair will determine the score he receives on the second bird.

If the gunner doesn't shoot at that first proof pair bird, the second bird will be scored as missed, whether he hits the second bird or not.

Always shoot at both birds of a proof pair.

That is about as complex as things get. Approach each station with confidence. Remember, this is a game of deception, of varying trajectories and angles, not of overpowering speed and incredible distances. Every shot can be made.

Naturally, it's best if someone else has the opportunity to apply that sort of positive thinking to the shattering of clay before you step in the cage. Without appearing too duplicitous, let someone else go first. You may be unnerved by watching too many shooters at a station, but you'll be ahead of the game watching at least one.

If everyone at the station plays "After you, Alfonse" and there's no getting out of being the leadoff hitter, take a deep breath, stand behind or to the side of the cage (it's against the rules to view a target from inside the cage), and call to the trapper for a view pair.

He'll holler back when he's ready. When you're prepared to watch, call "Pull!" or, better yet (in deference to our feathered friends), "Bird!"

IN THE BUTT
◆

Okay, you've seen it. You know where the trap is, what sort of targets are being thrown and how many, where they might be broken, and at what range. You know if the station is a timed reload. You know if the pair is simultaneous, on report, or following. So get on with it. If you have a bunch of choke tubes with you, pick a pair you think will work, but don't spend hours fretting over whether or not you should use skeet and skeet or cylinder and skeet. Err on the side of the more open choke for now.

Select the shells you think will work best: nines for close birds, eights for anything else. If one target is way out there—it shouldn't be, but sometimes it is—try seven and a halfs for that shot. Retrieve your gun from the rack, break it, and step into the cage.

If the station is one with a timed reload, you'll want to line up a dozen shells within easy reach. The extra two are to be used when you bobble and drop a couple, as you inevitably will. Most cages at timed reload stations have a shelf for this purpose. Stand the shells base down; if the shelf sports drilled holes in which you can stick your shells, use them. Make sure, however, that your shells don't bind in those holes when you pull them out at an angle, as you are apt to do in the fury of shooting.

If the station doesn't have a timed reload, you'll call for each pair of targets, so you can leave your shells in your vest or shell pouch.

Before you do anything, run down all the variables that will determine when and where you shoot:

A timed reload station. The shooter has set up more than enough shells to cover the ten targets.

- ◆ Poison birds.
- ◆ Location of the trap.
- ◆ Type and number of targets thrown and their paths.
- ◆ Best place to break each target.
- ◆ Second bird simultaneous, following, or on report.
- ◆ Timed reload or on command.
- ◆ Wind, visibility, background.

Your analysis of these factors will tell you how to stand and which target to take first. Many shooters like to take a minute to visualize the path the birds will take, watching in their mind's eye as they mount, swing, and dust each in turn.

Assume a good ready position with your lead foot pointed at the spot where you want to hit the first bird. Practice mounting your

Good foot position in the butt.

gun a few times, if you wish. Are there branches in the way? Will the cage prevent you from swinging on a bird? Will a black bird disappear against the background? Now is the time to adjust for those factors.

When you're ready, slip in two shells and close your gun. Safety on. You're going to break both birds, remember. There is no doubt in your mind.

Quickly review the way pairs will be thrown. Don't get caught flat-footed on a simultaneous release because you were expecting a report pair. Sometimes a station will alternate between simultaneous pairs and report or following pairs: a pair together, then a pair on report. Know which is coming first by asking the trapper or watching the first shooter in the butt. And if the station throws more than two targets simultaneously, simulating, say, a covey flush of quail, decide which two targets you'll go for and stick to your decision.

Remember that clay targets decelerate from the moment they're launched. The pigeon, when you first see it, will be going faster than it will be when you mount your gun and shoot at it. Remember, too, that as the bird nears the end of its path it will be dropping—faster than you think.

Now twist your head a bit toward the trap that will throw the first

A good ready position. The gunner's left foot is pointed toward where he wants to break the target. He has rotated his body to his right, in the direction of the trap. The gun is close to level, and he is looking over the muzzle.

bird. Your eyes must pick up the target first; your hands will follow and the gun will tag along. Your belly button should still be pointing toward the spot where you will take the bird. The muzzle of the gun should be on, or close to, that line and below your line of sight. The gun shouldn't be cocked up at an angle. The heel of the butt should be under your armpit. You should be relaxed, comfortable, and alert.

Remember—there may be a delay of up to three seconds from the time you call for the bird to the moment the trapper throws it, so don't be caught.

Okay. In a strong, confident voice call out "Trapper ready?"

The trapper will reply "Ready."

Now call for the targets: "Pull!"

THE SHOT

◆

The targets will be a pair, on report.

The first bird is launched. Pick it up with your eyes. Concentrate. As you follow the target, try to bore a hole through it as if you were Superman and possessed X-ray vision. Your gun will start its swing as you mount it, the left hand leading. Be positive now, in attitude, and swing.

When the gun hits your shoulder and your cheek comes firmly to the stock, focus your eyes on the target, fire, and swing through.

"Dead," calls the scorer. And seconds later, "and lost."

THE BIG MISS

◆

You got the first one—a cream puff right to left quartering shot—but the second bird, a hard-charging crossing shot, left to right, got away from you. Or to be more precise, you got away from it.

118

A clean gun mount insures a good shot. In the last picture, the gunner has fired and blinked, just as the camera was triggered. There is little variation in head position through the mount and the shot.

Here's what happened. After you popped the first target, your eyes strayed for a moment to admire your handiwork. *Say, we're pretty good at this,* they said. You may have picked your head up a bit for a better view. About then, the second bird appeared in your peripheral vision. You were no longer at your ready position, as you'd practiced, with the gun tucked under your arm; instead, you were looking down the barrel with your head cranked higher than it should be.

I can handle this, you thought. You started your swing, left to right, with the muzzle of the gun tracking the bird. You were locked on the target's trajectory, swinging through to overtake it. Looked very good. But then you passed the point at which you wanted to hit that bird. Better swing a little faster, try to catch up, you thought. Here we go. There's the bird, just off the muzzle. Passing, passing . . .

Oh no, said your eyes, as they dropped down to the barrel, that looks like too much space between the muzzle and the bird.

STOP!

The gun screeched to a halt as you pulled the trigger, and the bird sailed off into the sunset.

It's never as easy as it looks.

That second bird is the killer, remember. Not the shot, necessarily, but the very presence of the thing. It starts you thinking too much. It adds pressure. It flusters you.

It also makes the game.

DOUBLES DECISIONS
◆

You have to make several decisions on doubles, and they're not all simple. First, you must decide which bird to take first. That decision is made for you on following pairs or report pairs; you take the bird you see first. (You won't see the second bird on a report pair unless you shoot at the first!) But simultaneous pairs—targets launched at the same time from the same or different traps—pose problems.

There are a few rules of thumb to help you make a choice. These rules are predicated on two immutable facts: you must strive for unobstructed views of both birds without lifting your head from the gun; and you must shoot both birds before they crash into the trees, hit the ground, or sail out of range.

Therefore:

On a simultaneous pair of targets that stay together like a fighter pilot and his wing man, there's a great temptation to shoot for both birds with one shot. Don't fall for it. Pick one target, just as you pick one bird out of a covey, and stick with it.

- If the birds are launched from the same trap and are flying on parallel courses, take the trailing bird first. That way, your gun will continue its swing through that first bird (Bang!) and on to the second. Neither bird is blocked from your sight.
- By the same token, take the lower bird first. Again, you swing through the lower bird (Bang!) and move on toward the upper bird without interrupting your swing or blocking your vision.
- Take the bird to peak or die first, first. This rule can negate the

previous ones. If the leading bird runs into a tree thirty yards from the trap, you'd best take a stab at it. That's an extreme example. More often, this rule applies to birds launched from different traps. Go for the one that will smash up first.

There are several other bits of advice that may or may not apply to each pair of targets.

- If time allows, consider bringing your gun back to a ready position between the first and second bird. You can follow a bird with your eyes more effectively and get the gun on it faster from a ready position than with the gun mounted to your shoulder. With the gun mounted, you'll be tempted to lift your head to see the second bird, too, and lifting your head often guarantees missing the shot.
- If you don't have time to return to a ready position, don't lift your head from the stock to admire your handiwork on the first bird. This takes discipline and practice, but it will pay off.
- Don't rush, but take the first target quickly so that you have plenty of time for the second target—time enough, perhaps, to return to a ready position.
- On the second shot, let the bird do the traveling, not the gun. If the first shot is quartering away, left to right, and the second is crossing, right to left, there is a point somewhere in front of you where the paths of the birds may nearly cross. Take the first bird close to that point. The second bird will then travel close to where your gun is pointed. You can smoothly pick up the target, swing through, and kill it.
- Shoot before targets peak and before they start to drop. Tracking a target that has lost all its aerodynamic stability is difficult. The exception to this rule is on incoming birds that drop in front of you, targets that simulate decoying ducks. These birds are usually thrown from distant traps. When you first see them bearing in, they're often out of gun range. They won't come into range, in fact, until they start to drop. Therefore, you'll have to take them on the way down.

◆ If you miss the first target, stick with it and shoot at it again. Don't be distracted by the second bird, and don't swing on it if you missed the first target. Fifty percent of a pair is better than nothing at all.

◆ If you hit both targets with the first shot, shoot the second shell at whatever bits of clay remain in the air. This accomplishes two things: the second shot keeps you from breaking the rhythm of shooting twice, and, should there be some question as to whether or not both birds were hit, the second shot—if it's on—will administer a *coup de grâce* to whatever pigeon parts are still airborne.

◆ Pay particular attention to the type of pigeon presented. Battues should usually be taken just as they flare but before they drop (they're heavier than standards and drop like lead leaves). Minis and midis are fast out of the trap but decelerate more quickly than standards, and they're never as far out as they look. Remember, rabbits decelerate rapidly because of friction created between them and the ground. Swing with them, but not past them. Shoot low on rabbits, too, so your view of them is unobstructed and you can adjust to their course at the last minute should they hit a stone and bounce up in the air. Shot that hits the ground below a rabbit will ricochet up and break it.

◆ If you break the first three pairs, bear down. Most shooters lose concentration during the second half of a station. A. J. Smith tells of missing the last bird of the last pair at the last station in a hundred-bird shoot. He'd killed every bird until then. It's enough to make you cry.

SOME MORE THOUGHTS ON THE MYSTERY OF LEAD
◆

Lead, I told you in chapter 5, need not be consciously calculated. Some would say I lied. I couldn't argue with them.

The truth is, everyone perceives wingshooting differently. The instinctive method works very well for first shots, for birds within thirty yards, for targets quartering away, and for most shooters most of the time. There are occasions, however, when you may need a more refined system.

Specifically, on fast crossing birds, on distant birds, on the second shot of doubles when the gun is already mounted and you must come from way behind the target, a variation of instinctive shooting—pass through—may be most effective.

This is not to say that you should make a mental shift of gears. There is some magic in shooting objects out of the air. What works for one gunner fails miserably for another. I feel that instinctive shooting works on most shots and provides a solid framework of gun mounting and sighting techniques to apply to those targets that may demand a trifle more lead, and therefore more calculation.

Experiment with this. If swing through—tracking behind the bird, following its exact course, then pulling through it and firing as the muzzle swings by—works for you, use it. Let the British shooting maxim "Butt, belly, beak, bang" be your guide. As your gun is mounted, it's swung by the bird's butt, through its belly, past its beak, and shot.

Both instinctive shooting and swing through demand that you concentrate on the target, not on the gun; that you maintain a smooth swing; and that you pull through the target and not slam on the brakes when you fire. I believe the differences between the two schools are more of perception than of practice. Swing through acknowledges the presence of the rib and front bead in your secondary vision. You know they're there, but you don't focus on them. Instinctive shooting dispenses with all talk of secondary vision. Yet you still know where the gun is in relationship to the target because the gun is in your hand, and your natural hand-eye coordination tells you when the two are lined up.

Swing through gives your eyes two jobs: tracking the target with primary vision and the muzzle with secondary vision and relaying to your brain when the two are in the proper relationship for a hit. Instinctive shooting assigns the first task to your eyes and the second to your hands.

On hard crossing shots, you may want to try swing through. For that matter, you may want to try it on all shots. There are no absolutes. In fact, several accomplished sporting clays competitors use a version of sustained lead. At least that's how they describe what they see and think when they shoot.

Sometimes I wonder if trying to describe shooting things out of the air is not a bit like those blind men trying to describe an elephant.

The system you use is up to you. And the way to find the system that suits you best is to go out and shoot. Practice. And shoot some more.

◆

Enough generalities. In the next chapter we'll look at a sampling of sporting clays shots, stations that represent some of the more common layouts. All of the general guidelines we've talked about so far should apply. In fact, they should apply to any sporting clays station.

Following these guidelines won't always lead to success, any more than not following them will ensure failure. The unpredictability of sporting clays guarantees that. If we get axiomatic about a particular type of shot, a good course designer need only change things around some to take the wind out of our sails. We figure out one station and Poof! the next day it's gone. The only answer is to shoot and shoot and shoot, until you've seen all there is to see.

And then one will come along you haven't seen yet.

And that's as it should be.

7

A Sporting Sampler

◆

No target is easy until you hit it.
—A. J. "Smoker" Smith

They go by many names: bolting rabbit, bounding bunny, cackling rooster, curling pheasant, darting dove, driven pheasant, flighting mallard, flushed chukar, flushed pheasant, fur and feather, lonesome dove, mother chukar, pheasant over, pigeon and dove, prairie chicken, quail to cover, quartering away, rat and bat, rat and raven, ruffed grouse, run rabbit run, settling in, snipe away, Spanish partridge, springing teal, timberdoodler, vermin and vulture, widgeon, woodcock in cover, wood duck, and wood pigeon.

They are, as you may have guessed, the stations you'll encounter on a sporting clays course. The list of cute monikers may run out someday (I hope), but the variety of targets thrown from station to station and course to course never will. A rat and bat in Georgia will never be the same as a rat and bat in California or Maryland or New York.

For that matter, the Georgia rat and bat won't be the same in January as in August, in the morning as in the afternoon, because of all the variables: light, weather, wind, trapper reaction time, foliage, angle of the sun, and on and on.

Advice about shooting a particular type of station can thus only be given in general terms. To say you should shoot rabbits (or incoming, crossing, quartering, or dropping shots) in a prescribed manner not only takes the fun out of a station, but also does you a disservice. There are no absolutes here. What often distinguishes a great sporting clays gunner from a mediocre shot is his or her ability to factor those variables, devise a plan of attack for a station, and implement that plan with confidence.

Having said that, I'll now offer a sampling of eight stations, variations of which you'll encounter on most sporting clays courses. I'm contradicting my own advice against specifics because some explicit recommendations about stations is reassuring, particularly to the new sporting clays shooter. The stations I've selected appear everywhere (in various guises) because they're fun, because they take advantage of the inherent flexibility of traps and the variables of targets, because they represent the flight or running characteristics of several popular game species, and because they cover the basic angles: straight on, straight away, quartering, and crossing. The advice in this chapter provides a loose framework of techniques. It won't always work, although much of what I say is so universally accepted that you can apply it with some confidence when all else fails. But if you miss, don't blame me.

RABBIT

The rabbit will intimidate you first time up. Few of us are experienced at swatting things on the ground; even those who are—rabbit hunters, for example—blanch at their first encounter with a fur and feather station, which presents a bouncing bunny followed by a flying bird. This is mixed-grill gunning at its best.

Shooting into the dirt also has a strange psychological effect. We

A rabbit station. The target has been thrown from the brush pile to the shooter's left. Note how the gunner leans into the shot to keep his muzzle down.

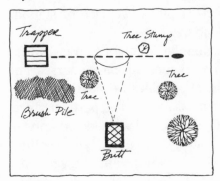

bear down on the earth and feel unsafe, so at the moment of truth, we lift the gun's muzzle. This habit is universal; almost all new sporting clays shooters fire high on rabbits their first time in the box.

Most of us also have trouble swinging through on a rabbit. The rifleman syndrome probably plays a role here. Creatures on the ground are to be aimed at, so we aim and stop and fire.

And miss.

Rabbits are not that hard. Although a rabbit may get off to a fast start, the friction he encounters when he hits the ground slows him down rapidly.

There are two keys to hitting rabbits: shoot low and swing through. You can force yourself to shoot low by shifting more weight to your front foot. Some shooters exaggerate this weight shift

128

by leaning well into the shot. Another suggestion is to extend or pull back your forward hand. Churchill advises the latter, explaining that retracting the forward hand will cause "tip-catting," a novel British term for muzzle drop on the mount of the gun. Many American shooters I've spoken with favor the opposite approach, however, extending their lead hand far out the fore-end. This, they tell me, puts more control in that lead hand and enables them to hold the muzzle down. Try both; one's bound to work for you.

Shooting low is advised not just to keep you from shooting high. Shot that hits the ground underneath a rabbit will bounce up and break the target much of the time. The army gives the same advice to infantrymen: aim low and count on the ricochets.

Rabbits are the most unpredictable of targets. One will run out smoothly, while the next will hit a pebble and jump two feet. If such a hop is a regular occurrence at a particular station, many shooters prefer to take the rabbit at the peak of its bounce, where it's visible and momentarily incapable of further erratic behavior.

Before you step into the cage, decide where you'll take the rabbit. Some stations offer only a small window through which the target may be shot. If that's the case, you'll have to get on the rabbit quickly.

You can see where your shot hits on a rabbit station, or at least you'll think you can. Inevitably, the puff of dust kicked up by your shot will appear to be behind any target you fail to break, even if you shot in front of the bunny. Don't fall into the trap of increasing your lead with each miss, based on your interpretation of that spout of dust. It always looks as if it's behind the rabbit because by the time the dust cloud registers, the rabbit has bounced well past where the shot hit. The relationship, then, between bunny and dust is deceptive. Remember, the rabbit doesn't demand much lead. You'll shoot over it and in front of it much of the time.

Getting back to the second target is often the most difficult part of a rabbit station. If you swing back to the trap, stop, pick up the second target, reverse your momentum, and swing through once again, you'll look like a carved figure on a cuckoo clock, choppy and awkward. The secret is to let the second target catch up with the gun, then smoothly follow through and fire. If time permits, consider coming back to a ready position between shots.

The Shot: Figure 1 shows a double rabbit, a fur and fur, with the second target released on report. The trap is to the left, behind a brush pile. A tree some fifteen feet in front of the trap prevents the shooter from engaging the target before that point. A large stump some thirty feet from that tree occasionally intercepts the target and powders it. The tree and stump, then, define the shooting window through which the gunner must engage the target. The rabbit's course runs from left to right, about twenty yards from the butt. The gunner has selected skeet and skeet for his choke and number-eight shot.

Note from the picture how the gunner exaggerates his forward lean to keep from shooting over the target. On his call of "Pull!" he picks up the target out of the trap with his eyes; when it clears the tree, he mounts his gun smoothly and smartly and creams the bird. For his second shot, he moves his gun slightly to the left, picks up the rabbit as it passes, follows through, and shoots a few feet to the right of where he took the first target, but before the rabbit can crash into the stump. A quick pair; off to a good start.

CROSSING
◆

You'll find an infinite variety of crossing shots in sporting clays: left to right, right to left, simultaneous pairs, pairs on report, and criss-crossing shots, with one from the left and one from the right. The possibilities are endless.

The most common crossing shot, however, is a simultaneous pair or report pair thrown from the same trap. Obviously, the birds may come from the left or from the right. Those thrown from the left are, in theory, a bit tougher for a right-handed shooter than for a lefty, because a left to right swing tends to pull the gun away from a right-hander's face and out of alignment with his eyes, while a right to left swing pushes the gun firmly into his cheek. Conversely, a left-hander will have more trouble with a bird thrown from the right.

Crossing shots rarely fly out of range, but they do crash—into trees, stumps, brush, and the ground. You have to pay close attention to timing on crossing shots, carefully selecting the point at which you'll engage the target.

On a simultaneous release, you'll normally take the rear bird first, then track through to the leading bird. This order insures that both targets are always visible. If the targets come out together, take the lower bird first.

An exception to that rule may arise if the lead target is on a course for a tree. Then you must take the lead target first, pause to wait for the second target to pass through, pick up your swing again, and shoot the second bird.

There is more talk of lead on crossing shots than on any other type of shot. Lead talk can be a deadly trap. A lead one gunner calls three and a half school buses (school buses, Volkswagens, and ducks being the standard units of measurement for lead) might appear to another shooter as little more than daylight. Everyone perceives lead differently. The only way to come to terms with lead is to shoot and shoot and shoot. Eventually, you'll devise a system, often instinctively, that will enable you to calculate lead.

The Shot: Figure 2 shows a simultaneous pair, crossing from left to right. The targets are twenty yards from the butt. They travel down a gully, so the gunner must pick them up against a background of dirt. As on the rabbit target, the gunner is shooting into the ground on this shot, and he'll have a tendency to shoot over the bird for the same reason: he'll see the ground and instinctively raise the muzzle of his gun.

The gunner selects cylinder and cylinder chokes and steps into the butt. He notes several trees to his right that might block his shot if he fires in that direction, so he decides to be aggressive and take

A crossing shot. The birds pass from left to right, down a gully in front of the gunner. He must shoot both before they're intercepted by the trees.

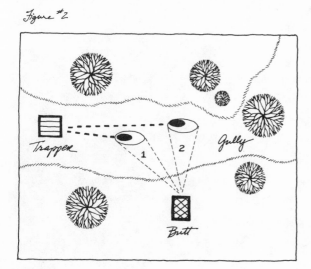

Figure #2

the targets directly in front. He points his lead foot in that direction, cranks his eyes and upper body toward the trap to the left, and calls "Pull!"

The pair is split high and low, with the top bird leading the lower bird by four feet. The gunner tracks the targets for a moment with his eyes. As he mounts his gun, he pulls through and fires on the trailing, lower bird, continues his swing through to the leading bird, and takes it ten feet before it can smash into a maple.

DRIVEN
◆

Incoming birds that pass overhead, thrown from a tower or high ground, imitate pheasant or grouse driven by beaters toward the gunner. When the birds come in low, you presume they're grouse; when they come in high, pheasant.

This is a very British presentation, since true driven shots are rare in this country. Upland gunners will be intimidated at first by

A driven shot. Nothing is more intimidating than a sixty-foot tower. The gunner is taking a bird directly overhead. Note how he has shifted his weight to his back foot and risen on the toe of his lead foot.

Figure #3

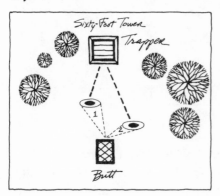

the angle of the bird and by its aggressive approach; I know I was. Waterfowlers are less in awe, because they often shoot at passing birds approaching at altitude.

In truth, this is often an easy station. Unlike ducks or geese or driven pheasant, the clay pigeons are decelerating. By the time they reach you, they're floating vulnerably. And instead of presenting a hard, narrow side view, they will have turned their soft underbellies to the gun. An incoming bird can provide an impressive, powdery hit. Misses are just misses.

Because the underside of the target will be exposed, light shot and open chokes are the norm. Use eight or nine shot and cylinder or skeet 1, unless the birds are high.

Often you'll spot the birds from a great distance. There's a temptation to mount the gun immediately and begin a long track of the targets, like an anti-aircraft gun in a World War II movie. Hold off. Track the birds with your eyes, determine which to take first, mount the gun smoothly, and shoot.

If you miss, stay with that target and shoot again. If you hit the bird, you must get on the second target quickly, before it gets by you. You may be able to wheel around and shoot behind you on a driven shoot, but in sporting clays, the cage should prevent such a maneuver; if it doesn't, a concern for others' safety surely will.

If the birds split, you'll need to change your footing. After the first shot, move your lead foot to point at the second target. If you have time, you may want to bring your gun back to a ready position. When swinging from one high target to another, you can twist so much that you'll cant the gun as you come through the target or pull the gun away from your cheek, both of which inevitably yield misses. By dropping the gun to a ready position and remounting, you'll be assured of a firm mount. Move your feet and try to keep your shoulders level.

There are two schools of thought about weight shift on high overhead birds. The first advises a shift to the rear foot. As the bird approaches, you move your weight to your back foot and simultaneously rise slightly on the toe of your lead foot. The other school advises keeping the weight on your lead foot and arching your back. Try both. Choose the method that feels comfortable.

The Shot: The gunner in figure 3 stands sixty-five yards from the trap, which sits high in a tower. The view pair told him that the birds will come in split: the lead bird to the left, the trailing bird slightly to the right of head-on. He decides to take the left bird first to give him some time to swing over to the second bird, even though swinging to the right (for a right-handed shooter) tempts his face to come off the stock. The shot will be taken at twenty-five yards, calling for cylinder and cylinder. He chooses number eights.

After his call of "Pull!" the gunner watches the birds approach. He doesn't mount his gun until he's ready to shoot. When the left bird is in range, he mounts his gun, blots out the target, and fires.

He then moves his lead foot toward the second bird and brings his gun on line with the bird. He swings through, shifting his weight to his back foot, and takes the bird overhead.

TEAL

◆

Springing teal targets are birds thrown from a trap set at a very high angle. They explode straight up like the waterfowl after which they're named. The trap is usually situated in front of the shooting butt or slightly to one side.

The trap or skeet shooter has never seen anything like this before, and most hunters are perplexed by the sight of a target screeching straight up, like a space launch. Throw in a pair of midis, which are particularly fast out of the blocks, and you have a devilishly hard shot.

You must remember that birds are at their maximum speed coming off the trap. Although you can spot teal targets as they rise out

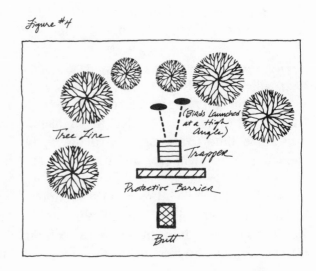

Figure #4

Tree Line

(Birds launched at a high angle)

Trapper

Protective Barrier

Butt

A springing teal setup. Note the high angle of the trap and the midi targets. These 90-mm pigeons are fast out of the trap. Their smaller size will fool a shooter into thinking they're farther away than they are.

A springing teal station. The targets erupt into the air like a space launch. With a dark background of trees, this gunner has a hard time picking up the birds before they reach the skyline.

of the trap, getting a gun on them at that point is virtually impossible. The solution is to engage the targets as they approach the apex of their flight, but not after they start to fall. A falling bird has the erratic aerodynamics of a fluttering leaf. In addition, coming down on a target as it falls is a particularly hard shot, compounded by the fact that as you pull through the target, the gun blocks it from your view.

Getting the jump on teal, then, starts with a proper stance. The gun should be pointed slightly up toward the area where you'll engage the target. Your eyes should be on the trap, ready to track the birds from the moment they launch. The mount should come just before the targets are taken, in good wingshooting style—not when the birds first appear, which would necessitate a long, awkward track of the targets.

The key to choosing where to shoot the first bird lies in how much time you have to get on the second bird. If the birds are a simultaneous pair, as is often the case, the first bird must be taken early so you can get on the second bird before it starts to fall. Timing is everything.

Remember, too, that the second bird will have lost more speed than the first bird and may start on its descent by the time you fire. It's all too easy to shoot over the second bird in a pair of teal.

The Shot: Figure 4 shows a station featuring a pair of midis launched out of a woodpile fifteen yards in front of the butt. The midis come out so fast that they'll be thirty or thirty-five yards in the air before the gunner can engage them. Thus, he selects improved cylinder and improved cylinder for chokes, with number eights.

On the call of "Pull!" the midis head for space. They're very difficult to spot against the dark background of trees until they lose some speed and appear against the sky. The gunner takes the lowest bird first, then swings over to the top target, which is near its peak. On the first pair he swings his muzzle through the second bird and shoots over it. On the second pair he fires under the second bird. The shot catches up to it on its descent.

DECOYING
◆

Incoming targets that land in front of the butt simulate ducks or geese landing amid decoys in front of a blind. For the waterfowler, this is a common shot; for the upland gunner, it's a novelty.

There are several mistakes made when shooting this presentation. The first is shooting too soon. Often the birds are visible when they're well out of range. The temptation is to mount the gun early and track the birds all the way in. Once the gun is up, however, the temptation changes. Now you want to shoot the birds while they're still on a level path. More often than not, at that point they'll still be some distance away. Better to wait, even though waiting means taking the birds as they stall and begin their descent.

There are two things to remember about descending targets. First, they will often tip an edge and sideslip, presenting a shot that is descending and moving laterally. Second, their descent is slowed by the cushion of air trapped beneath them. Dropping targets don't require much lead.

The Shot: The butt in figure 5 sits in front of a small pond. The trap is located off to the right, high on a ridge, and the trapper is throwing standard targets with a timed reload. The view pair shows that the birds crest over the trees surrounding the pond at a high altitude, then drop quickly to the pond. The water is thirty yards in front of the butt—a tough, long shot. The gunner selects improved cylinder for both barrels, lines up a dozen shells on the edge of the butt, and calls for the first target.

On the first pair, the gunner fires at the first target just as it stalls

A decoying station. The birds come in high, then drop into a small pond thirty yards from the shooting butt. The first bird is barely visible as a speck on the skyline above the pond.

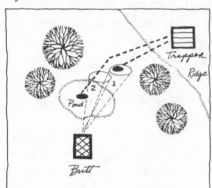

and begins to fall. He kills it but has difficulty pulling down on the second bird as it drops into the pond. He misses that shot.

On the second pair, he takes the first target earlier, which gives him more time to swing onto the second target before it drops. Because this is a timed reload, there is little chance for analysis between shots. And since this is a station that has several variables that demand close scrutiny before the gunner decides how to take the targets, the first shooter in the butt is at a distinct disadvantage.

OVERHEAD

◆

Any course that has a high tower will want to use it in as many presentations as possible. The obvious choice is to throw high driven birds that come directly at you. The more difficult shot, however, involves birds thrown from behind you or to the side, birds that scream overhead and away like passing ducks.

The tower provides the altitude; the proximity of the tower to the butt provides the speed. You must pick up the target quickly, mount your gun smoothly, come from behind the bird and through it, then fire before it's out of range. If the butt sits to the side of the tower, rather than directly beneath it, the difficulty of the shot is compounded, for you'll have to compute movement in two directions: away from you and crossing in front of you.

To shoot a station like this using lots of mental calculations is nearly impossible. But by trusting your instincts, by having faith in your natural pointing ability, you can make this shot more often than not.

The secret is to shoot the bird quickly, before it travels far enough to push the range of choke and shell. Start with your weight on your back foot and muzzle up toward the area where you'll engage the bird, your head and eyes cranked toward the trap. As with incoming targets, overheads present their vulnerable underbelly to you, so breaking the clay is not as difficult as it may look. Have confidence. Try not to be intimidated by the tower and the speed of the targets on release. Remember, they're slowing down with each millisecond.

The Shot: The gunner in figure 6 stands to the left of the tower. The view pair showed him that the birds are a report pair. The first bird is more of a crossing shot; the second takes a course straight

An overhead station. Although this looks like a terribly difficult shot, basic wingshooting techniques will break target after target. The key is to get on the bird quickly.
In the photo on the left, note that the gunner is cocked back toward the tower with his gun muzzle up, ready to swing, mount, and fire the moment the target appears. The photo on the right shows that the shooter has mounted his gun quickly, while the target is still overhead presenting its vulnerable underbelly.

Figure #6

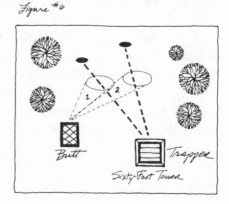

out from the tower. The gunner selects improved cylinder chokes for both barrels and number-eight shot.

He points his lead foot at an area between his position and the trap, where he plans to take the first bird. He rotates his upper body to the right and shifts most of his weight to his back leg. Raising the gun's muzzle slightly above horizontal, but not so high as to block his vision, he calls for the bird.

As soon as his eyes lock on the bird, he begins his mount. The bird is moving quickly, but as he follows it with his eyes and upper body, the motion is transferred to the gun. His weight shifts to his forward foot. As soon as the gun hits his shoulder, he swings through the bird and fires.

On the second shot he shifts his lead foot more toward the trap, brings his gun back down to a ready position, and transfers his weight back to his rear foot. The bird is thrown. The gunner mounts, pulls through, and fires. Two kills. When asked by his shooting partners how much he led the targets, he says he saw no lead at all.

QUARTERING
◆

Birds that fly neither head-on nor straight away, neither left to right nor right to left fall into the great void known as quartering. Quartering targets may be angled toward you or away from you. To compound the difficulty of this presentation, the target may quarter-in or quarter-out at a high angle, a low angle, or on a flat trajectory.

Quartering shots can be simple or difficult, depending on the variables. Because the speed of the target and the angle of its approach may vary, generalizing about quartering shots is tricky.

Quartering shots are best taken quickly, before the bird gets out of range or passes you. Most quartering shots require little lead. A good smooth gun mount with your eyes locked on the target will impart enough swing to the gun to break most quartering shots, provided you don't slam on the brakes at the moment of the shot.

A quartering shot. This deceptively simple shot can throw the best shooters for a loss. The left photo shows the bird quartering in at a high angle from the left. The gunner shot at it as it began to fall over the trees on the far left side of the field. When that failed, the gunner took a different approach, canting his gun to track the rising bird (right photo). Canting enabled him to approach the target as a simpler crossing shot. His lean allowed his gun to rise with the bird as he swung through it.

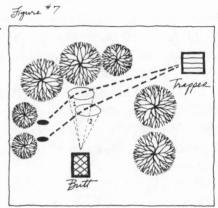

For every simple quartering shot there is a devilishly difficult one. If the trap is ten yards to the side of the butt and ten yards behind it and the target is thrown straight out in front of you, the shot is easy. But if the trapper moves to a different location, raises the elevation on the trap, and cranks up the spring, a quartering shot can confound the best. Let's look at a particularly tough shot.

The Shot: Figure 7 shows the trapper located in trees and brush off to the right. The view pair shows a following pair launched on a quartering-in course at a high angle. The birds skim over the tops of the trees in front of the trap, rise at high speed to the top of the trees on the opposite side of the field, then quickly lose their speed, dip a shoulder, and tumble to earth. The problem is that the birds are rising and crossing at the same time and don't come into range until they're very near the peak of their flight and ready to drop into a dipsy dive toward the earth.

The gunner chooses skeet and skeet for this shot. The targets are thirty yards or so out, but because they are showing a bit of under-belly on their high angle, the shooter decides to err on the side of a more open choke.

On his call of "Pull!" the first bird launches. The gunner pauses to wait for it to come into range. As it approaches the peak of its flight, he mounts his gun. The bird begins to fall. The gunner swings down on the bird, pulls past it, and shoots under it. He misses the first bird.

The second bird is thrown. This time the shooter decides to take the bird well before it peaks. Unfortunately, the diagonal course of the bird confuses him. The bird is rising, crossing, and coming toward him. Another miss.

On the second pair the shooter takes yet a different approach. He decides to minimize the confusion imparted by the bird's rising trajectory by bending to the right from his waist. This cants his gun so that a plane drawn through the two barrels would be perpendicular to the path of the targets. In effect, this canting enables him to view the bird as a crossing shot. His swing from right to left will rise with the birds because of the lean in his body.

On most shots, canting the gun is bad form, but it can be effective on this type of target. And here it is. The gunner takes the first target at the peak of its flight, the second just before it drops. "Shoot them like crossing shots," he says. And he does.

FLUSH

A flushing shot, which is thrown from a trap in front of the butt, presents two or more targets heading away from you. Often the birds have a low trajectory, like a covey of quail. The shot is straightforward enough, if there are no obstacles in the way, but the obstacles are usually there.

Often more than two birds are thrown, so you have to decide which pair of birds you'll shoot before you step into the butt. Multiple targets are usually set up so that one of the birds must be taken quickly, while it is still clipping along at a fast pace. The second bird, however, will have slowed down considerably by the time you get on it, and it may be dropping when you fire.

The Shot: The trap in figure 8 sits behind a pile of brush twenty yards in front of the butt. The targets are a simultaneous pair, with one bird going to the left, one heading straight down the line. The gunner selects cylinder and cylinder chokes and number-eight shot. He plans to take the left bird first, for a tree lies in its path and that bird will inevitably smash up if he doesn't take it immediately. He knows this is the epitome of instinctive shooting; a clean mount and confidence will enable him to run ten targets straight. He also knows that an early miss on an easy target will so demoralize him that he'll be hard-pressed to recover for a decent score.

He calls "Pull!" The birds launch. They're more difficult to see against the background of trees than he thought they would be. He

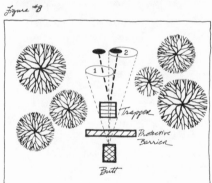

A flush station. The flush is so simple it will get you time and again. A smooth, fast mount is the key to getting on the bird quickly. The decision about which bird to take first is best made before you step into the butt.

takes the first bird handily, but by the time he gets on the second bird, it's thirty-five yards away and pressing the limits of his open choke. He fires. A piece of clay chips out. The bird's a kill. He knows he should have selected a tighter choke for the second shot, but it's too late now. Out of the next eight targets, he kills six. The two misses are on the second bird. So it goes.

◆

That's a fair sampling of what you'll see on an average sporting clays course. Since I've mentioned only eight targets, you know you'll see at least two other variations of these shots on a round of ten stations. There's a chance, too, that you'll see something entirely new, something that tests you, that demands you return to the basics of good wingshooting (the foundation of this sport), a target so inventive that it mimics the challenge of real hunting.

8

Variations on the Theme

◆

To ride, shoot straight, and speak the truth.
—Charles T. Davis, *For a Little Boy*

BACKYARD CLAYS

◆

My friend Bob Philip, who works at Orvis, lives in Danby, Vermont. Danby is not a typical American suburb, nor is Bob's backyard a typical American suburban backyard. Bob owns about five acres of hardscrabble countryside, with stands of pine and fields of puckerbrush dotted with crab apples and barberries. I'd be tempted to poach grouse in Bob's backyard if I didn't think I'd be shot.

But I probably would be, not out of malice (well, maybe not), but because Bob shoots sporting clays there all the time. From what I've seen and heard, Bob's Sporting Clays, as that piece of Danby real estate is known, may be as good—if not better—than a lot of commercial setups.

What I particularly like about Bob's is its flexibility. With three or

Sporting clays is a fine introduction to shotgunning for kids. This is midwinter gunning practice in Vermont—the sport transcends the seasons.

four Trius traps and a couple of commercial manual traps, Bob can throw about any target known to man. He doesn't have a tower, I know, but he does have a steep bank. By putting a trap on top of the bank and the shooters at the bottom, Bob can throw a driven bird that is good enough to beat me about eight out of ten times.

In England, I'm told, it's not uncommon for a gang of men to knock on a farmer's door, ask permission to set up a range in his field, haul out three or four traps and some hay bales to protect the trapper, and have an afternoon shoot. When the day is done, the traps go in the boot and the shooters go home.

I like that system. With one commercial manual trap and two or three Triuses, I believe an inventive soul could present any conceivable target, depending on the terrain and vegetation.

Here are a few things to consider if you're interested in setting up a backyard course:

- Safety is all-important. A commercial trap can throw a bird more than a hundred yards; that's about the range of number eights, too. To be safe, make sure there is nothing in your line of fire for at least a hundred and fifty yards. Two hundred yards is even better.
- Protect the trapper. Hay bales are used on many commercial courses. They are readily available and relatively easy to lug about. Stick them in trash bags and they'll weather at least one summer. Insure that you have enough, that you stack them high, and that the trapper has sufficient sense to stay behind them. The trapper must always wear glasses, too.
- Even with protection, never set up a trap that might come under direct fire. It isn't necessary.
- Insure that the trappers know the calls. Always ask "Trapper ready?" Don't load up until you hear a response.
- Be respectful of the neighbors. Don't shoot at the same location week after week if the noise might bother folks. Use common sense and practice common courtesy.
- You can get a commercial trap to throw rabbits or you can build a simple chute down which a bunny can roll. Lay out a piece of carpet for ten feet in front of the trap and smooth out the rest of the ground over which the bunny runs. Give him a bush to duck behind. Compensate for lack of speed by showing the gunner the rabbit for only a brief time. And when he shoots, fire off an aerial. You can mount a Trius vertically and install a target stop (a rubber-covered pin to position the bird) and a strong teal clip (a length of wire to hold the bird on the arm), and the trap will throw rabbits.
- White Flyer is coming out with biodegradable targets. Ask your

*A wire arm, called a teal clip, holds a target on the throwing arm
when the trap is set at a high elevation.*

local sporting goods store to check on their availability. Standard
targets are not really dangerous (except to hogs, which eat
them), but they are unsightly.

◆ Make a cage out of PVC or metal conduit. Cart it from station to
station.

◆ Midis off a Trius will sail almost as fast and as far as standards
from a commercial manual trap.

◆ Use the terrain. Brush, washes, gullies, hills, and ponds all offer
variations that make for interesting stations.

◆ If you shoot regularly at a commercial course, never tell your
shooting partner that you have been practicing at home. But
don't be afraid to make a small wager on your ability at the
course after several weeks of home improvement.

152

FITASC

◆

FITASC stands for Fédération International de Tir aux Armes Sportives de Chasse; that translates to the International Federation of Sporting Clays. FITASC, which is used as an acronym and pronounced "Fee-task," is the governing body of this sport on the world level.

FITASC sporting is a variation of sporting clays that is popular in Europe and, to some degree, in England. We'll be seeing it in the States some; we'll certainly be hearing more about it.

A FITASC course or layout, as it is called, consists of four or five traps. Around this layout are three or four shooting positions.

On the first round of FITASC, the gunner loads two shells and enters the first shooting position. He is then presented with a number of single targets thrown from any of the traps on the field. He may shoot twice at each single.

After the shooter's squad has rotated through the single presentation, the first shooter goes back on line at the same position and is thrown doubles. He only can fire two shots per pair.

When all the members of the squad have shot at the doubles targets from station one, the group rotates to the next station and goes through the lineup again. The leadoff position at the second station goes to the second man on the squad. First single birds are thrown to each shooter, then doubles are presented.

The squad works around the field in this manner. Each succeeding station is more difficult than the last, for although the gunners shoot at birds from the same four or five traps, the course is designed so that changing angles and obstacles increase the complexity of the shots.

In all, twenty-five targets are presented to each shooter at each layout. A good score is twenty or better.

A competition consists of two to eight layouts for a total of fifty to two hundred birds.

A FITASC layout presents more specialty targets to a gunner than a standard sporting clays course, which is restricted to throwing specialties no more than 30 percent of the time.

FITASC layouts rely on automatic traps operated from a control station. Therefore, the investment in setting up such a course is far greater than that for a sporting clays field. To my eye, at least, the game holds more appeal for the target shooter than for the hunter. We'll have to see if it catches on.

JUST WHO IS THE WEAKER SEX?
◆

It all depends on who isn't shooting particularly well on a given day.

The few comments I have on women and sporting clays reside back here not because I'm a chauvinist swine, but because I have very little to say. Shooting in general, and sporting clays in particular, knows no sex barriers. Everything I said in the front of this book holds for both women and men.

If there are any special considerations for the female shooter, they are as follows:

◆ More women have eye dominance problems than men. Why, I don't know; I'm not sure anyone does. But the folks at the Orvis school, who have tested thousands of men and women over the years, tell me this is true. So women should test themselves for eye dominance (chapter 5) before they start shooting.
◆ Women with small frames may have difficulty buying a gun off the rack that fits. Most over-the-counter shotguns are built for Joe Average. He's five-ten and 170 pounds. The stock on such a gun will probably be too long for a woman. The barrels may also be too long, throwing the weight of the gun too far forward for someone weighing 120 pounds. The pitch won't be great enough

A woman's only handicap in sporting clays is a husband who insists on teaching her.

to conform to a woman's shoulder and chest. And the gun may be too heavy.

The solution is to be fitted properly and either order a custom gun or have a stock gun altered. Since removal of material is usually the answer, most gunsmiths, even those without a try gun and fitting experience, can get you in the ballpark by cutting down barrels and stock and adding three or four degrees of pitch.

◆ Recoil can also be a factor, particularly for a woman who's just getting started. Many experienced female shooters handle recoil as well as any man, regardless of their size and build.

Recoil can be tamed in several ways. A lighter gauge is the first solution. A sixteen- or twenty-gauge firing one-ounce loads is quite effective for sporting clays. Don't go to a twenty-eight, however; the penalty in less lead is too discouraging for a beginning shooter.

A gas-operated automatic lessens kick perceptibly; a gas-operated twenty with target loads has virtually no kick at all. Women who have had some shooting experience can usually shoot a twelve-gauge automatic without difficulty.

Lighter loads in a twelve-gauge are the next step, along with backboring the barrels and lengthening the forcing cones.

♦ Learn the basics of shooting and safe gun handling from someone other than your spouse. (This applies to both sexes.) A couple of hours with a qualified instructor is far cheaper than a divorce lawyer.

That's about all the quasi-technical advice a woman needs.

The only real disadvantage a woman has in any shooting game is men's longstanding belief that shooting is something only men can do. That philosophy has scared off many a woman.

It simply isn't so, as a number of women have proven lately on sporting clays courses around the country. There need be no handicapping of sexes in this game. If the top women shooters lack anything, it's simply time behind the gun.

With decent instruction, beginning women often shoot better than men who are new to the sport, because women don't step behind a gun full of preconceived notions about wingshooting distilled from a childhood of blasting Indians with cap guns.

Last winter I shot dove with my friend Sally Kleberg Espy down in Texas. Sally grew up on the King Ranch. She learned to use a shotgun—and a horse—the way most of us learned to use a knife and fork. Sally can shoot the eyes out of birds. Suffice it to say, Sally limited out and still had shells from her first box jangling in her pocket.

I didn't have to worry about jangling shells. Nor did I fret over cleaning a limit of dove that day.

There's no way I wouldn't give Sally a handicap at sporting clays. In fact, I'd glue full chokes tubes in her gun if I could.

THE FUTURE OF THE GAME
◆

There are some sure-money bets that I'd make on this game. We'll see more people shooting smaller gauges. We'll see competitions for side-by-sides. We'll see more courses open and some shut down because of noise, because of lead, because shooting is still seen as a scary, violent activity by some.

We'll see biodegradable clay targets that will make casual backyard shooting less messy and commercial operations less labor-intensive. We may see steel shot mandated for sporting clays courses, because communities and zoning boards are already questioning the effects of lead concentrated on a small piece of the earth. (At the 1989 USSCA National Championship, competitors spread about three tons of lead over a few acres in two days of shooting. That may have an adverse effect we should address.)

I believe large numbers of hunters and fair numbers of new shooters will take up sporting clays, as long as the sport does not take a hard turn down the road to competition. I hope that's the case.

I believe I'll never get very good, never better than average, but I also believe I might outshoot you (if you're average), while hunting my birds—grouse and woodcock—in my own backyard.

And now, I believe I've said enough.

Appendixes

◆

A. OFFICIAL RULES OF THE NSCA
◆

The rules of the National Sporting Clays Association and the United States Sporting Clays Association are nearly identical. There are only three major distinctions:

1. The NSCA permits gunners to shoot reloaded shells; the USSCA prohibits the use of reloads at the upper echelons of competition.
2. The NSCA permits two malfunctions in gun or shells in one day. The USSCA rules say that a gun or ammo malfunction is tough luck; the target is scored as lost.
3. The NSCA permits gunners to change chokes between stations; the USSCA says chokes may be changed only between fields, a field being one or more stations serviced by the same trap.

If you're a recreational shooter, as I am, don't be intimidated by all these guidelines. Should you read them, you'll note a lawyer's deft touch, which is to say that many paragraphs describe simple courtesy and common sense. It is the shooter's responsibility to keep his scores during the year and reclassify if necessary to a higher class. A shooter may not go down in class until year end.

◆

The following is an informative summary of the organization of the National Sporting Clays Association. The official National Sporting

Clays Association rules govern the shooting of registered targets, the conduct of shooters, and the duties of shoot management. The NSCA has the responsibility for the formulation, regulation, and enforcement of these rules.

The NSCA reserves the right to make alterations in, or amendments to, these rules at any time, whenever it deems it to be in the best interest of the National Sporting Clays Association.

GENERAL INFORMATION
◆

A. PURPOSE OF NSCA
The purpose of the National Sporting Clays Association is to promote and govern the sport of sporting clays throughout the United States and Canada. The NSCA is dedicated to the development of the sport at all levels of participation. We vow to create an atmosphere of healthy competition and meaningful fellowship within its membership. We also offer the hunter a recreational target shooting game, which will strengthen his hunting and gun safety skills and extend his shooting season.

B. MEMBERSHIP
Annual membership dues are thirty dollars a year with a copy of the official monthly magazine, *Sporting Clays, The Shotgun Hunter's Magazine*. A twenty-dollar membership is available to dependents (no magazine).

The membership and shooting year is from January 1 to December 31.

Application for annual membership may be made at any registered shoot by filling out an application or by contacting the NSCA for an application.

C. CLASSIFICATION
1. Lewis Class: After reviewing all forms of classification, the advisory council recommended the Lewis class system for classifi-

cation, mostly because of the wide variations of difficulty level for range layouts. This system is based on the final scores as they are posted when the shoot has been completed and gives every contestant an equal chance to win, no matter what his shooting ability.

Until we have a fair track record on course layout, this system is highly recommended. This does not mean we are forcing you to use this system, but only the recommendation of the council. See the later section on the Lewis class system.

2. Blind Draw: In using this system, management decides which fields are to be used. Generally, this system uses half the fields shot during the event and the total score from those fields are added together and multiplied by two (2). This figure is then used on a classification table to determine the shooter's class for that day's shooting.

3. Stencil System: This system also takes into account half the targets shot during the event. Several basic rules apply to this system, such as:

a. Cut out 50 percent of the shots per field but never use the first two shots.

b. Shoot management should not disclose this stencil to any participant.

c. As shooters finish, take the overlay stencil and place it on the card and add all hit targets and multiply by two (2).

This will give you the average, which can be used with the classification schedule to assign a class for each shooter.

4. Average Method: The average method is yet another way of classifying and the following rules apply:

a. A new shooter will attain his classification after shooting three hundred targets. He will reclassify after each three hundred targets—at six hundred targets, nine hundred targets, etc.

b. Shooters must always reclassify at the end of each regular string (three hundred targets) even though the correct number of targets for reclassification comes between the preliminary and the main event. Reclassification is not effective until AFTER the shoot, but must be accomplished on the correct number of targets.

c. During the current year, a shooter is subject to reclassify UPWARD ONLY.

d. Reclassification DOWN will only be accomplished by NSCA at the beginning of the next sporting clays year. However, you may only go down ONE CLASS.

Class	Averages
AA	75 and above
A	65–74.99
B	55–64.99
C	54.99 and below.

D. RULES OF CONDUCT OF NSCA SHOOTERS

Each member will be furnished a copy of these official NSCA rules, with the understanding that the member will read and understand each rule. Members are strongly encouraged to know these rules and abide by them, both for their own benefit and for the benefit of other shooters.

By entering the competition, every person agrees to accept all official decisions and to abide by these rules.

When making your entry at any registered shoot, produce your plastic identification card and your average card so that your name, address, and membership number are properly noted and errors in records prevented. Shooters not having their plastic cards should always list their NSCA number, entire name, and address on the event cards.

The scorecard is intended for the purpose of providing the classification committees at the shoots with up-to-date data on your shooting ability. Shooters not having their cards up-to-date may be put in a higher class or otherwise penalized.

It is the duty of each NSCA member to have his/her average card updated at the end of each shoot.

Failure to accurately record scores, or the falsification of scores, can lead to suspension from the NSCA.

E. CONCURRENT EVENTS

Concurrent events will be offered in:

Lady-Junior-Senior

Junior-any person who has not reached his eighteenth birthday.

Senior-any person who has reached his sixtieth birthday.

The Advisory Council is considering the possibility of adding other concurrent events. Pending results, shoot management may offer other concurrent categories, such as Sub-Junior, Sub-Senior, Sub-Sub-Senior, and Veteran.

F. TOURNAMENTS

Only clubs affiliated with the NSCA shall be eligible to conduct registered shoots.

Only members in good standing who have paid their annual dues may participate in registered NSCA shoots.

RULES AND REGULATIONS
◆

I. Definition of Terms

A. SHOOT PROMOTER

Individual(s) or entity that provides for the facilities and organization of the competition. Shoot promoters may also act as shoot officials.

B. Shoot Officials

Individual(s) appointed by the shoot promoter and responsible for course layout, target selection, and appointment of field judges. Shoot officials shall be responsible for both layout and testing of the course. Shoot officials are responsible for ensuring that competitors are not allowed to test or preview the course prior to the competition.

C. Field Judges

Persons over eighteen years of age assigned by the shoot officials to score targets and enforce the rules.

D. Station

A shooting position from which one or more targets are attempted.

E. Field

A station or group of stations from which targets are attempted sequentially. Once a squad or individual checks into a field, all stations and/or all targets on the field are attempted before moving to another field. The shoot officials will provide direction for execution of shooting at each field.

F. Report Pair

Two sequential targets where the second target is launched at the sound of the gun firing at the first target.

G. Following Pair

Two sequential targets where the second target is launched at the officials' discretion after the first target.

H. Simultaneous Pair

Two targets launched simultaneously.

II. Equipment

A. Targets

Targets thrown in any event may include any or all of the following:

Appendixes

1. Regulation skeet or trap targets as specified by ATA, NSSA, or ISU.
2. Mini, midi, battue, rocket, or rabbit targets as specified by FITASC.
3. Propeller mounted ZZ-Pigeon targets.
4. Any sporting clays target approved by shoot officials.
5. Poison bird targets of a separate and clearly discernible appearance may be included at random. Shooters attempting shots at these targets shall be scored a miss or lost bird. Shooters correctly refraining from attempting the poison bird (protected species) will be scored as a hit or dead bird.
6. Target number and selection for any competition shall be at the discretion of the shoot officials. No more than 30 percent of the total number of targets shall be other than targets described in A-1. Target number and selection shall be the same for all shooters.

B. Shotguns

1. Shotguns of twelve gauge or smaller gauges, in safe working order and capable of firing two shots, are to be used in attempting all targets.
2. Shotguns fitted for multiple barrels (of various chokes and/or lengths) are permitted. The shooter is allowed to change barrels only between stations or as otherwise directed by the shoot officials.
3. Shotguns with interchangeable or adjustable chokes are permitted at the shooter's discretion. Chokes can be changed only between stations or as otherwise directed by the shoot officials.
4. Competitors may enter a shoot with various guns and attempt targets at various stations with different guns or the gun of another competitor. Guns may be changed only between stations or as otherwise directed by the shoot officials.

C. Ammunition

1. All shot shell ammunition including reloads may be used. Shoot officials may further limit the ammunition to be commercially manufactured.

2. Loads for twelve-gauge guns shall not exceed one and one-eighth ounces of shot charge.
3. Maximum shot charge for any given competition may be further limited by the shoot officials.
4. Shot size shall not exceed U.S. number seven and a half (diameter 0.095"; weight 1.07 grains).
5. Shot shall be normal production spherical shot. Plated shot is permitted.

D. THE COURSE

1. The course will provide for a predetermined number of shooting fields from which each competitor will attempt various targets. The number of stations and the number and characteristics of targets from each station, on each field, will be determined by the shoot officials, and will be the same for all shooters.
2. Targets will be propelled by, and launched from, any of a number of commercially produced, modified, or handmade devices, which will propel an approved target in a manner to approach the characteristics (in the opinion of the shoot officials) of a game bird or animal typically taken by a sporting shotgun.
3. Launching devices that provide for targets traveling at varying angles and distances to the competitors are acceptable (i.e. wobble traps). No more than 20 percent of the targets shall be presented from such devices. No less than 80 percent of all targets in a shoot shall be presented with a reasonably consistent trajectory, distance, and velocity to all shooters.
4. Devices that provide for propelling multiple targets are permitted.
5. Devices propelling targets of more than one type, and devices capable of providing targets at varying angles and distances, shall be employed only as the varying aspects of these devices will be the same for all shooters and will be free of all human element of selection.
6. Field judges will be required at each station in sufficient number to competently enforce all rules for the shooter, as well as to

score the attempts accurately. Numbers and positions for field judges shall be determined by the shoot officials.

III. Execution of the Shoot

A. SHOOTING ORDER

Contestants shall proceed through the course and competition in one of the following formats:

1. European Rotation: Individual competitors or groups of two through five competitors will proceed to the various stations. Groups may shoot in any order selected by the shooters. The squad or group shooting the stations of any field may be changed from field to field.

2. Squading: At the discretion of the shoot officials, groups of three to five shooters will be formed to proceed from field to field in a fixed sequence.

3. In European Rotation, a shoot start and shoot end time will be established. It will be the responsibility of each shooter to complete the entire event between these times.

4. In squading sequence, squads will be assigned a start time, and it is the responsibility of each shooter to be ready on time, or within no more than five minutes of that time.

5. In either case— shots not attempted by the shoot end time (European rotation) or shots not attempted by the shooter joining his squad after they have begun (squading)—those targets not attempted will be scored as lost. The shoot officials shall have the right to provide for makeup targets if sufficient justification can be presented. Makeup targets are provided solely at the discretion of the shoot officials.

6. Rotation of Order: In squads of shooters, rotation of shooting order is permitted between stations. Rotation may be formatted by shoot officials, to be followed by all squads. If not prescribed by shoot officials, order will be determined by shooters.

7. Shooters Viewing Targets: There will be no view targets for any shooter on station. In the instance of the commencement of shooting, or if no station has had a contestant on the line for fifteen minutes or longer, targets may be presented for viewing from locations normally accessible to spectators.

B. ATTEMPTING TARGETS

Targets will be presented for attempt at each station in one or more of the following formats.

1. Single Target/Single Shot

2. Single Target/Two Shots The target will be scored hit or dead if successfully attempted on either shot.

3. Doubles/Two Shots: Doubles may be presented as report, following, or simultaneous pairs. In simultaneous pairs the shooter has the right to shoot either of the targets first. If the shooter has missed the first target he may fire the second cartridge at the same target.

When shooting report or following pairs, the shooter will have the right if missing the first target to fire the second cartridge at the same target (the result being scored on the first target and the second target being scored as lost).

Should the shooter break both targets with either the first or the second shot, then the result will be scored as two kills.

4. Multiple Target/Two Shots: Two hits or dead birds maximum.

5. Stations at which the shooter is walking are permitted. (See section VIII-C.)

6. Time Reloads: Targets presented with set time periods for shooter to reload prior to the presentation of the subsequent targets are permitted. Five seconds is the normal reload time but other intervals may be used at the discretion of the shoot officials.

IV. Rules for the Shooter

A. LOW GUN

Gun stock must be visible below the shooter's armpit.

B. Call for Target
Target will be launched immediately or with a delay of up to three seconds.

C. Mounting of Gun
Shooter is to keep from mounting his gun until target is visible. If in the judgment of the field judge the shooter moves to mount his gun prior to seeing the target, the target will be a no bird and the sequence and call will begin again. No penalty will be assessed the shooter. Excessive no bird (three per day) can be construed as cause for scoring targets as lost.

D. Shooter's Responsibility
It will be the responsibility of each shooter to be familiar with these rules. Ignorance of the rules will not be a cause to re-attempt targets lost because of rule violations.

V. Scoring

A. Targets shall be scored as hit or killed or dead and designated on scorecards by an X when in the opinion of the field judge a visible piece has been broken from the target. Targets not struck and broken by the shooter's shot shall be called lost or missed and designated on scorecards by an O.

B. The call of lost or dead, hit or miss, shall be announced by the field judge prior to recording the score on every target.

C. If the shooter disagrees with the field judge's call, he must protest before firing at another set of targets or before leaving that station. The field judge may poll the spectators and may reverse his original call. In all cases the final decision of the field judge will stand.

D. Each shooter will be assigned a scorecard to be presented to the field judges at the various stations or fields. Field judges will score each shooter's attempts on the individual's scorecard. The total shall be tallied and the scores written in ink and initialed by the field judge.

E. Each shooter is responsible for his scorecard from assignment, at the start of the shoot, until the card is filed with the shoot officials at the end of each day's shooting.

F. Shooters are responsible for checking the field judge's totals of hits and misses at each station and/or field.

VI. Malfunctions

A. SHOOTING MALFUNCTIONS

The shooter shall be allowed a combined total of two malfunctions per day attributed to either the shooter's gun or ammo. Targets not attempted due to a third or later malfunction shall be scored as lost. Targets not attempted on the two allowed malfunctions shall be treated as no birds.

1. Gun Malfunctions

a. In the case of a gun malfunction, the shooter must remain in place, the gun pointed safely downrange, and must not open the gun or tamper with trigger, safety, or barrel selector until the field judge has determined the cause and made his ruling.

b. Targets shall be scored as lost if the shooter is unable to fire because of the following. Examples include but are not limited to:

1. Shooter has left the safety on.
2. Shooter has forgotten to load or properly cock the gun.
3. Shooter has forgotten to disengage the locking device from the magazine of an automatic weapon.
4. Shooter has not sufficiently released the trigger of a single-trigger gun having fired the first shot.

c. If the shooter fails to comply with item VI-A-1-a, the target or targets will be scored as lost or missed.

170

2. Ammo Malfunctions

a. In the case of an ammunition malfunction, the shooter must remain in place, the gun pointing safely downrange, and must not open the gun or tamper with the trigger, safety, or barrel selector until the field judge has determined the cause and made his ruling.

b. Examples include, but are not limited to:

  1. Failure to fire, provided firing pin indentation is clearly noticeable.

  2. One in which the primer fires, but through failure of the shell or lack of components consequently leaves part of or all of the charge of shot or wad in the gun. A soft load, in which the shot and wad leave the barrel, is not a misfire.

  3. Brass pulling off hull between shots on doubles.

  4. Separation of brass from casing when gun is fired (usually accompanied by a whistling sound as the plastic sleeve leaves the barrel).

c. If the shooter fails to comply with item VI-A-2-a, the target or targets will be scored as lost or missed.

B. TARGET MALFUNCTION

1. A target that breaks at launching shall be called a no bird and shooter will be provided a new target.

2. A target that is launched in an obviously different trajectory shall be called a no bird and the shooter will be provided a new target.

3. If a bad target or no bird is thrown on the second target of a double, and if the shooter has already attempted the first target prior to the field judge's call, the attempt on the first target will be recorded as fired. The complete double will be repeated; however, the first target of the pair will remain as

scored and the proof double will be thrown only to record the attempt on the second target. The shooter must make an attempt at both targets. Failure to make a legitimate attempt on the first target shall be cause for scoring the second target as lost.

4. If a bad target or no bird is thrown during a timed reload sequence, the shooter will repeat the sequence beginning with the last target established.

    As in the proof double described in VI-B-3, the shooter must make an attempt at the established target before proceeding with the remaining sequence. If the last established target occurred before the timed reload, the shooter shall begin the sequence accordingly and proceed through the reloading again. The field judge shall enforce his judgment (either by implementing a suitable penalty or allowing a repeat of the reloading sequence) to prevent a no bird or bad target thrown after either a successful or an unsuccessful reloading attempt from changing the results of the initial sequence.

5. At a station of multiple targets, at least two good targets must be presented or a no bird will be called and the multiple targets will be attempted again. Multiple targets shall be shot as fair in the air, two new shots will be attempted and scored, no scores from previous no bird attempts will stand.

6. Any targets broken by another target, or pieces from another target, will be called a no bird and treated as per paragraph VI-B-3.

VII. Protests

A. A shooter may protest if in his opinion the rules as stated herein are improperly applied.

B. There will be no protests concerning calls or scoring of hits or misses. The field judge's final decision will stand.

C. Protests shall be made immediately upon completion of the shooting at a given field. Protest shall be made to the shoot officials.

D. The shoot officials shall convene a predetermined jury of three to five field judges or competitors who are known to be representative of the shooters present and knowledgeable about these rules. The jury will decide on the validity of the protest and the resolution of the case. They will prescribe penalties or award bonuses as they determine to be fair and in the spirit of the competition.

VIII. Miscellaneous

A. Safety is everyone's responsibility.

B. It is the shooter's responsibility to report any unsafe shooting condition immediately to shoot officials.

C. Stations at which the shooter is walking, setting in a blind and/or a boat, or any other situation other than the regular standing position are not recommended. These stands all represent a simulated hunting situation; however, large crowds are not present during this type of hunting. Safety is the number-one consideration for all sporting clays ranges.

D. Shooters must have the direct permission of a field judge to test-fire any gun. Other than on such permitted test firings, guns will be discharged only in attempts at competition targets.

E. Field judges may be assisted by markers to record scores on the shooters' scorecards.

F. It is the sole responsibility of the shooter to begin any event, station, and/or field with sufficient equipment and ammunition. Failure to do so, which in the opinion of the field judges will delay the shoot, will result in the loss of all targets as required to keep the shoot moving. Makeup targets will be provided only at the discretion of the shoot officials.

173

G. Formats for shootoffs to break ties shall be at the discretion of the shoot officials.

LEWIS CLASS
◆

This system has been in common use for a good many years as a method of dividing optional money. It is also popular in a good many sections of the country as a means of distributing prizes where the past averages or known abilities of shooters are not available.

This system is based on the final scores as they are posted when the shoot has been completed and gives every contestant an equal chance to win, no matter what his shooting ability.

Reminder: Classification has nothing to do with your class in the Lewis class. Your class for this event will be determined solely by the rules below.

When all the shooting has been completed, the scores are listed in numerical order from the highest to the lowest. They are then divided into as many groups as there are classes. For example, if there were sixty entries and four classes, there would be fifteen scores in each class. The highest score in each class would then be the winner.

Since there will often be odd numbers of entries and tie scores on the dividing line between the classes, the following rules have been established:

1. Where a short class is necessary, due to odd entry list, the short class or classes shall head the list.
2. Where the line of division falls in a number of tie scores, the contestants are assigned to the class in which the majority of the scores appear.
3. Where an equal number of tie scores appears on either side of

Appendixes

Scores and Lewis Classes

Brackets represent assignment of scores according to Rules 2 and 3. Horizontal lines represent division of all entries into classes according to Rule 1.

CLASS 1		CLASS 3	
180	Winner Class 1	162	Rule 2 places all
179		162	163s in Class 2
179		162	therefore 162s tie
178		162	for Class 3
178		162	
178		161	
178		161	
177		160	
177		159	
177		158	
176		157	
175		157	
175		157	
174		157	
174			

CLASS 2		CLASS 4	
173	173s tie	156	
173	for Class 2	—	Rule 2 places both 156s
172		156	in Class 4 and they are
170		154	tied for this class
170		153	
169		150	
168		149	
167		149	
167		148	
167		147	
165		146	
164		145	
163		144	
163		144	
163		140	
—		140	
163		139	
		135	

the line, contestants shall be assigned to the head of the lower class.

4. Where the original division is changed, due to tie scores, this change shall apply only to the classes directly affected and the original division shall continue in the other classes.

To cite an example, we will take a shoot containing a two-hundred target program in which there are four Lewis classes and sixty-two contestants. Since the short classes are placed first, there would be fifteen shooters in Classes 1 and 2 and sixteen shooters in Classes 3 and 4. The final scores are arranged from highest to lowest and the lines drawn in between the classes.

B. ORGANIZATIONS
◆

There are two groups dedicated to promoting sporting clays and to maintaining records of shooters and competitions. The USSCA in Houston was founded in 1987; the NSCA, based in San Antonio, has a more recent birthdate, but it's the offspring of the National Skeet Shooting Association, which has been around for seventy years.

The NSCA puts out a nice monthly magazine called *Sporting Clays, The Shotgun Hunter's Magazine.* One month the issue is devoted to sporting clays shooting; the next month the emphasis is on hunting.

The USSCA includes with its membership a subscription to *Shotgun Sports.* This monthly magazine, which has been around a long time, usually runs at least one feature on sporting clays and carries a newsletter from the USSCA, announcing rule changes and such.

You don't have to join either of these groups to shoot sporting clays. But to enter their tournaments or to receive a classification, you'll have to sign up. And you should. Both publications offer helpful information, and the membership fees are quite reasonable.

It remains to be seen if these two groups will continue as separate entities, like the WBC and the WBA, or will merge somewhere down the line.

National Sporting Clays Association
P.O. Box 680007
San Antonio, TX 78268
(512) 688-3371

United States Sporting Clays Association
50 Briar Hollow, Suite 490 East
Houston, TX 77027
(713) 622-8043

In Canada, contact:
Canadian Sporting Clays Association
882 Quest Road
Hemmingford, Quebec, Canada J0L 1H0
(514) 699-0879

C. ADDITIONAL READING
◆

There are lots of books available on shotguns—books on shooting, collecting, tinkering, and on the rich history and tradition of guns. There are even a few that get rather Zenlike in their approach to popping a few caps. Here are my favorites—those I believe you can't do without:

The Orvis Wing-Shooting Handbook by Bruce Bowlen (Nick Lyons Books, 1985; paperback). The most concise, authoritative book you can read on instinctive shooting and gun fitting. This is the curriculum of the Orvis Shooting School, written by a former director who just happens to be a good friend and the finest field shot I've ever seen. His dog isn't too bad, either.

Intensity at the highest level of competition: the USSCA National Championship.

Shotgunning: The Art and the Science by Bob Brister (Winchester Press, 1976; hardcover). This is the bible of American shotgunning. Brister actually had his wife drive around in the family station wagon towing a large sheet of paper so he could blast at it to test theories on shot strings. No one can pass up research like that.

Robert Churchill's Game Shooting by Robert Churchill and Macdonald Hastings (Countrysport Press, 1990; hardcover). Back in

178

print after a hiatus of many years, this classic British treatise on the Churchill Method, first published in 1955, is fascinating reading with an uppercrust lilt. Churchill and Brister should be on either end of your bookshelf.

Sporting Clays by A. J. Smith (Willow Creek Press, 1989; hardcover). A. J. "Smoker" Smith has become England's sporting clays ambassador to America. A superb sporting clays competitor, Smoker writes with charming humility for a man at the top of his game.

The Double Shotgun by Don Zutz (Winchester Press, 1985; hardcover). Development and history of American, British, and European double-barreled shotguns.

Best Guns by Michael McIntosh (Countrysport Press, 1989; hardcover). The further adventures of great guns from America, England, and the Continent.

D. SUPPLIERS
◆

For information on the Orvis Shooting School, their gun-fitting and gunsmithing services, and sporting clays traps, guns, and accessories, write or call:

The Orvis Company
Historic Route 7A
Manchester, VT 05254
(800) 548-9548

There are many good gunsmiths around the country who can alter your shotgun. Most of them advertise in either *Shotgun Sports* or *Sporting Clays* magazines. Two outstanding firms immediately come to mind. Both have well-deserved reputations for excellent work and relatively quick turnaround.

Pro-Port Limited
41302 Executive Drive
Mt. Clemens, MI 48045

Pro-Port can port barrels, lengthen and polish forcing cones, backbore, and rechoke your gun.

Briley
1085 Gessner
Houston, TX 66055

Famous for their interchangeable choke tubes, Briley can do about anything you might want done to your gun, too.

E. CLASSIFICATION
◆

Competitive sporting clays shooters are sorted into classes, so that the top guns don't shoot against those just entering the sport. Categories break out into letter designations: AA, A, B, and C; AA is the top of the heap.

A person must shoot a certain number of targets before he can be classified. Generally, once a shooter reaches a particular classification, he can't backslide into a lower rating. The particulars of how these categories are factored vary a bit between the USSCA and the NSCA. In the simplest terms, anyone who hits over 75 percent of his targets through the course of a year is an AA shooter. Break 65 percent in the NSCA or 70 percent in the USSCA and you're an A shooter. Hit 55 percent in the NSCA or 60 percent in the USSCA and you're a B shooter. C shooters are those who fail to make the B category, whether they shoot 54 percent or 4 percent.

Often these groups are further split into Ladies, Seniors (over sixty), and Juniors (under eighteen) classes. Some tournaments have a Hunter category with a lower entry fee for the more casual shooters.

Inevitably, classes for smaller gauges and for gunners shooting side-by-sides will appear at many shoots.

Glossary

♦

Automatic: A shotgun that fires a shell and chambers a new round each time the trigger is pulled.

Automatic Trap: An electric-powered machine for throwing clay pigeons that cocks and loads targets automatically. The trap is normally fired by a remote electric trigger.

Backbore: A gunsmithing technique to reduce recoil and improve patterning by enlarging the diameter of the barrel from the forcing cone to the choke.

Battue: A clay target 108 mm in diameter, lacking the pronounced dome of a standard. Heavier than a standard and less aerodynamic, battue targets fly erratically, particularly as they lose speed.

Bead: See Gun Anatomy.

Butt: See Gun Anatomy. Also, the shooting position on a sporting clays course (also called a stand or cage).

Cast: Lateral deviation of the gun stock from the long axis of the sight plane. Cast is a bend in the stock to the right (cast-off) or left (cast-on) of the long axis of the barrels.

Choke: Constriction of the inside diameter of the barrel at the muzzle. Choke controls the expansion of shot when it leaves the barrel.

Choke Changer: A tool for removing and inserting choke tubes.

Choke Tubes: Steel tubes that thread into the muzzle of a gun. Choke tubes come in varying diameters. By changing tubes, one can change the choke of the gun.

Churchill Method: A wingshooting technique, developed by the famed English instructor Robert Churchill, in which no lead is calculated. The gunner concentrates on the target, raises his gun, and fires the moment the butt is firmly mounted. The method is predicated on our natural hand-eye coordination and our ability to point directly at anything on which our eyes focus.

Clay Pigeon: An aerial target made of asphalt pitch and limestone, which shatters when hit by shot.

Comb: The top of the stock on which the cheek rests.

Cross-Dominance: A condition in which the dominant eye isn't on the same side as the dominant hand (a right-handed shooter with a dominant left eye, for example).

Delayed Launch: A trapper may delay up to three seconds before launching a clay pigeon from the time the gunner calls "Pull!"

Dominant Eye: The controlling eye. When one focuses on an object and then shuts the nondominant eye, the object doesn't move. When one shuts the dominant eye, however, the image shifts perceptibly.

Double A: The top shooter's classification in sporting clays. Also AA.

Double-barreled: A shotgun with two barrels, aligned horizontally (side-by-side) or vertically (over-and-under).

Doubles: Two targets thrown simultaneously, following, or on report.

Drop at Comb: The vertical distance from the comb of the stock to the plane of the sight rib.

Drop at Heel: The vertical distance from the heel of the butt to the plane of the sight rib.

Duo-Shot: A shotgun shell loaded with two different sizes of pellets.

Earmuffs: Sound-reducing ear wear, resembling cold-weather earmuffs.

Field: Two or more stations firing at targets thrown from the same trap.

FITASC: The international governing body of sporting clays, Fédération International de Tir aux Armes Sportives de Chasse. Also a type of sporting clays in which a variety of targets are presented at one station.

Following Pair: A pair of targets thrown in succession, the second lagging the first by several seconds.

Fore-end: See Gun Anatomy.

Grip: See Gun Anatomy.

Gun Anatomy:

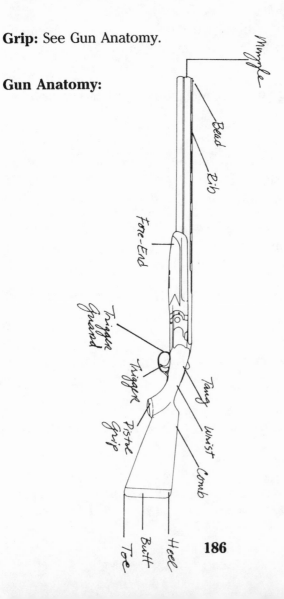

186

Hen Bird: A clay target that penalizes the shooter should he fire at it. Also called a poison bird.

International Standard: A standard clay pigeon measuring 110 mm in diameter, 2 mm larger than a sporting clays pigeon or a standard pigeon.

Manual Trap: A device for throwing clay pigeons that must be cocked and loaded manually.

Midi: A clay target resembling a standard but measuring 90 mm in diameter.

Mini: A clay target resembling a standard but measuring 60 mm in diameter.

NSCA: The National Sporting Clays Association, one of two organizations conducting competitions and classifying shooters in sporting clays (see USSCA).

Over-and-Under: A double-barreled gun with the barrels aligned in a vertical plane, one on top of the other.

Pattern: The distribution of shot at a given range, determined by shooting a shell at paper and noting the spread of holes.

Pitch: A measurement of the angle of the butt of the gun in relationship to the plane of the barrels. Pitch is measured in degrees of variation from a true right angle.

Poison Bird: A clay target that penalizes the shooter should he fire at it. Also called a hen bird.

Port: To port a barrel is to cut a series of small holes near the muzzle. These holes direct escaping gasses upward, stabilizing the gun and reducing recoil.

Pump: A shotgun in which a shell is chambered by sliding a handle, located under the barrel, backward then forward, like a trombone slide.

Quail Walk: A trail flanked by traps that can be triggered to release targets as a gunner walks down the path.

Quartering Target: A clay target thrown at an angle of approximately forty-five degrees to the gunner, either incoming or outgoing.

Rabbit: A reinforced clay target measuring 108 mm in diameter, which can be thrown to roll along the ground, simulating a running rabbit.

Report Pair: A pair of targets, the second thrown at the sound of the gunner's shot at the first.

Rib: See Gun Anatomy.

Rocket: A clay target about the size of a standard but more robust and therefore faster than a standard on launch.

Shoe Protector: A flap of leather that fits over the toe of the shoe to protect it from carbon from the muzzle of the gun.

Side-by-Side: A double-barreled shotgun with the barrels aligned in a horizontal plane.

Simultaneous Pair: Two clay targets thrown at the same time.

Spot Shooting: A wingshooting technique in which the gunner holds his shotgun steady at a point in front of the target and fires when he believes shot and target will collide.

Stand: The shooting position on a sporting clays course. Also called a cage or butt.

Standard: A clay target measuring 108 mm in diameter and having a pronounced dome. The standard is the target most frequently encountered.

Station: A shooting position on a sporting clays course encompassing the stand, the trap, and the area over which the targets will be engaged. Analogous to a hole in golf.

Sustained Lead: A wingshooting technique in which the gunner determines a specific distance to hold his gun in front of an aerial target and moves his gun with the target to maintain that distance.

Swing Through: A wingshooting technique in which the gunner tracks his target, then swings past it, firing as the muzzle passes the target by a predetermined amount.

Teal Clip: A loop of wire used to hold a clay pigeon on a trap arm when the trap is elevated to a high angle. Without a teal clip, the pigeon would fall off.

Timed Reload: A shooting station at which birds are released one after the other, without waiting for the gunner to call "Pull!" The gunner is forced to reload quickly between the release of pairs.

Trap: A device for throwing aerial targets.

Trapper: A trap operator.

Trigger: See Gun Anatomy.

Trigger Guard: See Gun Anatomy.

USSCA: The United States Sporting Clays Association, one of two such organizations in the United States (see NSCA).

View Pair: A pair of targets thrown for each new group of shooters at a station to show them what to expect at that station.

Wobble Trap: An automatic trap that oscillates to throw successive targets in different directions and at varying angles.

Wrist: See Gun Anatomy.